C0-DKN-124

SEARCHING FOR FAITH WITHIN A CONFUSED SOCIETY

Dennis A. Anderson

SEARCHING FOR FAITH WITHIN A CONFUSED SOCIETY

Copyright © 1976 by
The C.S.S. Publishing Company, Inc.
Lima, Ohio

Second Printing 1984

All rights reserved. No portion of this book may be reproduced or utilized in any form or by any means, electronic or mechanical including photocopying, without permission in writing from the publisher. Inquiries should be addressed to: The C.S.S. Publishing Company, Inc., 628 South Main Street, Lima, Ohio 45804.

1903/ISBN 0-89536-206-6   PRINTED IN U.S.A.

This book is affectionately dedicated to my wife and children for their daily help in the search for faith and to the congregations who have given me the opportunity to share with them in the search for faith.

TABLE OF CONTENTS

INTRODUCTION

Martin Marty coined the phrase "religion in general" a number of years ago to describe the religious atmosphere of much of middle America. Since the 1950s, we have added to the gray layer of religion in general, other layers of religious experience. We have the dry digital layers of scientism of the years of the moon race, and the inspiring reds and blues and fluorescence of the Jesus and Spirit movements, and then cynical black of the Watergate days. Others better equipped than I can describe and chart the character of religion in America in the mid-seventies. But while that charting is going on, the struggle to find and define faith continues. That is what these sermons are about.

These sermons were written to meet several specific goals. At St. Paul's Lutheran, Grand Island, we established a number of spiritual objectives for the decade. Among them were these:

- To develop an awareness of the unique gifts of the Christian faith within the Lutheran tradition, and to become aware of the dangers of a weak and watered down cultural religion in general.
- To combat the "consumer, passive receiver," approach of a religion in general.

We have found that the Martin Marty description of faith in American culture still holds true for many. These sermons were delivered in an attempt to meet the religious confusion of our time and place. Perhaps they will be helpful to others in their search for a faith in a cynical society confused over what and how to believe.

— Dennis Anderson

(A special word of appreciation to Alice Bett and Helen Mader for their dedicated help in manuscript preparation! Willing workers are precious gems. Thanks!)

8

I.
Faith Is Possible, Even for Me

FAITH/LET GO AND LET GOD

Texts: Jeremiah 17:5-8
        1 Corinthians 15:12-20
        Luke 6:17-26

"Blessed are you poor . . . Blessed are you who hunger . . . Blessed are you who weep. Blessed are you when men hate you . . . woe to you that are rich. Woe to you who laugh . . . " (Luke 6:20 ff)

What in the world is Jesus saying? God blesses all those things of which we are afraid — poverty, hunger, sadness, happiness. He condemns the things we love — riches, full stomachs, happiness.

At first it sounds as if Jesus is saying, "If you're now poor, hungry, and sad, don't worry. Someday, in Heaven, you'll get your share. Everything works out." But then he says, "Woe to you who are rich, full, happy." Am I condemned just because I'm comfortable? What is Jesus getting at when he blesses hurt and condemns comfort?

Jeremiah gives us part of the answer. "Cursed is the man who trusts in man and makes flesh his arm, whose heart turns away from the Lord. He will become like a dried up desert bush." Scripture shows us how God reverses what we, as men, value as strong and important in life. Or, to put it even better, how we reverse what God says is really important. The beatitudes are a reversal of all the values by which we live. What Jesus blesses, we seek like the devil to avoid. We spend our lives trying to achieve what he condemns. "Trust in the values of man and you'll end up like a dried up desert bush, at the end of life, all washed up."

Focus on this business of reversing our values, turning our understandings and lives upside down. This is one of the reasons we have such a hard time believing. God's values are so different from ours! The contrast is devastating. So we run from God. There are five very popular misconceptions, or misunderstandings, of what faith really is.

Some people have faith in faith. Faith becomes some sort of magical religious power. We are exhorted, told over and over, "You have got to have faith." Faith in what? Often that doesn't make any difference, as long as you sincerely believe in something somewhere. Having faith in faith is like falling in love with love. There isn't much satisfaction there. You must fall in love with someone specific — blonde, brunette, tall, short. Likewise, your faith must be in someone specific.

For others, faith is a religious knowledge. Faith is knowing a lot about God, about Jesus, about the Bible. The Danish Lutheran theologian, Soren Kierkegaard, once told the story of a room with two doors. Over one there is a sign, "Lecture on Heaven;" over the other, a sign "Heaven." People flock through the door marked "Lecture." It's safer and easier to go to a lecture on Heaven, but it doesn't go anywhere. A lecture on love is not quite like falling in love.

Faith is ethical purity to many of us, a spotless life where all the enjoyable things are forbidden. Some of us tend to measure one's faith by his "goodness." "Oh, he/she was such a good person!" Karl Olsson, a former seminary professor, tells what many have experienced. Once in his youth, a pastor encouraged him to come to communion. He resisted, saying, "I'm not good enough." To which the pastor replied, "Moral worthiness is no prerequisite for receiving God's grace. Jesus prayed, 'Forgive them.' "

"You gotta have hope!" And that is right; but some people confuse hope with faith. By hope they usually mean blind hope, a wishing for the impossible. Faith is then a wishful thinking, a betting against the odds. Faith is being optimistic when all else is pessimistic. St. Paul said, "If we have only hope, we are the most pitied of people." Faith gives rise to hope. But hope is not the same as faith. Faith gives rise to an optimistic view of life because, by faith, we know God. But to make faith and hope the same is to reduce faith to no more than wishful thinking. "It won't rain, I hope, I hope, I hope."

To a large number of us, faith is "hanging in there;" faith is a religious muscle, a "spiritual endurance." We get a lot of stuff like "faith is when you reach the end of your rope — you tie a knot and hang on." Not bad advice for secular wisdom. But that is not necessarily faith.

"If you only hang in there, God will bless you." For example, football player Johnny Unitas, as a child, dreamed of playing for Notre Dame, but he was too small. In 1955, he was ninth-round draft choice of the Steelers, and was cut without ever playing. He tried the Browns, but Otto Graham came back from retirement. So who wants an unknown like Unitas? But, his rejection just fired up his determination and he finally made it! "Now that's faith."

That's hogwash! Faith gives endurance. But, how about the person who just can't hang in there any longer? Is he condemned? Is my own religious muscle and strength the measurement of my faith? If that is what my salvation in life depends upon, I've had it — because I'm not that strong.

Faith in faith, knowledge, moral purity, wishful thinking, endurance — these are all forms of our *own* power and strength. In fact, if our salvation depends upon any of these misunderstandings of faith, we are all going to end up like dried-up desert bushes. Jesus says, "Blessed are the hungry, the poor, the weak! Woe to the strong, the rich, the full!" Why? Because when we are strong and rich and full and everything is going our way, we are too tempted to trust in our strength and power and wit and wisdom. That won't cut the mustard of life!

We can believe in Christ intellectually.

We can admire him.

We can say prayers to him through the keyhole of life.

We can push coins at him under the door.

We can be moral and decent.

We can be baptized and confirmed, but still never open the door to him.

Why? Because we are trusting in ourselves. Most of us are terribly afraid of ever being needy. We don't want to need God. We want to be able to stand on our own two feet without accepting a handout or help from anybody. That is why Jesus says, "Woe to the rich, the full, the strong." That is why Jesus says, "It's harder for a rich man to get into heaven than for a camel to go through the eye of a needle." The rich are full of their own beans and never need to turn to God's meat!

Jesus is suggesting that faith is not something we possess of our own strength or power. Faith possesses and overwhelms us. Faith comes when you can't hang on to the end of the rope any longer. Like the man in the Old Testament saying, "Lord, I'm wearied with groaning. I soak my bed with weeping." Or like the man of today, saying, "I'm at the end of my rope, Lord. I'm shattered. I'm broken." Faith begins when we let go of the rope — and faith begins when we dare let God manage our living. For me, that's not easy to do. But it is better than just trying to hang on. Let go and let God in.

THE SURPRISING EXAMPLE OF FAITH

Texts: 1 Kings 8:41-43
       Galatians 1:1-10
       Luke 7:1-10

Jesus draws our attention to a Roman soldier, a captain of a Roman garrison in Capernaum. Jesus says of him, "I tell you, not even in Israel have I found such faith." It happens again. When Jesus is around, the unexpected seems to happen. Jesus points to a pagan, a foreigner, as the great example of great faith.

"Great faith!" Which one of us here this morning would not like to have the kind of faith this centurion had? Whatever Jesus said would happen, he believed, and obeyed without a single question. We need faith. We search for faith and, when it does not come, some of us simply give up and try to live without it. Anton Checkov, in his play, *Three Sisters*, has one of his characters utter the profound truth about life without faith in God. "I think a human being has got to have some faith, or at least he has got to seek faith. Otherwise his life will be empty, empty. How can you live and not know why the cranes fly, why children are born, why the stars shine in the sky? You must either know why you live or else nothing matters, everything's just wild grass." Here today and gone tomorrow and that's all.

Where is faith found? How is faith developed? The surprise in this gospel event is that Jesus points, not to the super-religious people as the examples of faith, but to one who appears to be, rather, a secular man of the world. Why? I would expect that the greatest faith would be found by those who were the most active and religious in the church. But here, Jesus says, "not even in Israel, among God's chosen people, have I found such faith as in this Roman soldier." Why is this secular man, rather than the religious man, the example of faith?

Let's talk a bit about being secular, worldly men, and religious men. I don't know which category you would put yourself in, but listen and see. First, we'll think about the secular man, the person who is outside any form of religion. It is rather easy to be that kind of person nowadays. Most people will say they believe in God, but intellectual belief and faith — those are two different concepts. Does the modern scientific man really need God?

Humanity has achieved the status of majority stockholder in the firm "Creation, Inc." Humanity has added an eighth day to the seven days of creation, and the new one is under our administration. The "Old Man," the boss is deposed, and his residence, called Heaven, is declared obsolete and torn down. We don't really need God for health, life, or salvation anymore, since we have gadgets galore and medical and scientific miracles in wide array and store, except, of course, in extreme emergency when the priests of science reach that rare moment when they can do no more and say it is "all in the hands of God."

The liturgy of the totally modern secular/worldly man is

> Glory to man in the highest,
> For man is the maker of gadgets.
> Hail to the unholy
> Who gives us that which we wish to get.*

The secular man would quickly reply, "Do I need God? No, I don't. My life is full without him." Such would be the description of the totally secular non-religious person. But I don't believe that describes me or too many of us here today. Nor would the description of the totally religous man of "great faith" describe too many of us.

My guess is that we fall somewhere inbetween men of great faith and men of the secular world. Maybe something like the fine member of the congregation who

*P. W. Turner, *Christ in the Concrete City,* © 1960.

admitted that he had begun to take long weekends at the lake. He said, "We began to wonder whether we needed church. At first we felt a little twinge of guilt not going to worship Christ. But you know, Pastor, life went on as usual. Our lives didn't fall apart." I strongly suspect that is where most people are. Kind of half-way inbetween. Faith and yet not great faith. Faith is not something which we lose, so much as we simply cease letting faith shape our lives and hopes.

Our religion then becomes one more compartment in our lives like Boy Scouts, clubs, work, home, and shopping. Our Christian faith gets reduced from being the very core of our lives down to a frosting on top of a too-busy cake. St. Paul describes this kind of religion in his letter to the Galatians. He is "chewing out" the Galatians for quickly backsliding and leaving behind the gospel of Jesus Christ for another gospel. Christianity had become, for the Galatian Christians, just another religion on top of their previous Jewish faith. Christianity is always in that danger in our lives, of being reduced to a sort of thirty-third degree Masonry, something that we add on top of an already too busy schedule, a cherry on top of the cake of life, rather than the very foundation of our hopes. Another way to put it, Christianity becomes a luxury option like airconditioning or automatic defrost of rear windows on our cars. We can really get along quite well without it, but we keep some faith around for emergency.

Now, some of us take God a little more seriously than this. We may not be halfway in between faith and no faith, but probably two-thirds faith (if you can speak in quantitative terms). Faith is pretty strong as long as things are going along fine. It is easy to have faith in a great God and sing, *How Great Thou Art* when you can look up at the night sky and see a canopy of diamond stars, or when you hear your first baby cry, or when there are miraculous healings. But, what about those long silent nights of the soul when we struggle for faith and nothing seems to be going right?

Can we continue to believe when God doesn't perform those miracles we hope for? When life seems one defeat after another?

For me, the gospel, the good news that Jesus shares with us in the event of this Roman soldier who becomes the example of great faith, is found in the surprises. We would expect great faith to be found in the temple of Jerusalem, among the great artifacts of the church, and in the great leaders of the church.

Jesus says, instead, that it was found unexpectedly in this man of the world who would take Jesus simply at his word and obey. So, maybe, just maybe, we look for God in too limited places. Chances are we'll look for God in the Bible and the creeds and places where he should be obvious. He is to be found there. Yet, maybe he is to be found not only among the things that are obviously religious, but in the dark tragic spots of life, in the bodies of children now — right now — starving in Africa and India, or in the grief of some widow next door to you who is alone.

And another surprise: Faith is not a great achievement reserved for the greats of religious past. Rather it is a gift open to all who ask. It was the Roman soldier who sent for Jesus. It was to him Christ came.

You know there is good news there for me, especially as I "flip and flop" between doubt and faith and struggle. Faith may not be found so much in great moral strength as in the struggle going on between God and me. Physicians tell us there is hope for a TB patient as long as he has a fever. It is when the body has given up and no longer struggles that death conquers. Faith is given in the struggle.

That's good news, at least for me, when Jesus points to the Roman soldier as the example of faith. If he who at one time was far out is now close in, there is hope for me if I will but ask.

Jesus, come to my house and heal.

REFORMATION AND PASTORAL CONCERNS

Texts: Jeremiah 31:31-34
       Romans 3:19-28
       John 8:31-38

This day is a great and historic anniversary day in the church. October 31, 1517, Dr. Martin Luther, a pastor, priest, and theologian of the church, nailed ninety-five articles of theological debate on the church door of Wittenberg University. The reforming light and power of the church was set aflame.

History has not been the same since, either for the religious or for the secular world. Usually on this day we recall the gigantic contributions of Martin Luther. We remember his translation of both the Bible and the worship service into the language of the people, his rediscovery of the central truth of the Christian faith — *Salvation by God's grace through faith alone.*

Ths morning, however, I'm not going to speak with you about the dramatic and the sweeping historical themes of the Reformation, significant as they are. Instead, I'm simply going to share some pastoral concerns, pastoral concerns not about the reformation of the church, but more personally about the spiritual renewal of the life of our own congregation. Martin Luther was not only a theologian struggling with the historic issues of the church, he was a pastor who spent much time preaching, teaching, and calling upon his flock. The heart of the Reformation, the foundation of the church, is that we know Jesus as both Savior and Lord — and as a result, our lives are reformed. This then, is not an event of nearly a half-century ago — or two thousand years — but an event which must occur for us in our day.

Death claims all of us, said Luther. *And every-one must die for himself. I cannot be with you and*

*you cannot be with me. We may shout in each
others' ears, but each man must stand on the
ramparts of death alone.*

No one can die for you. No one can live for you. No
one can believe for you. This is the first pastoral concern
I share with you. There are some of us who expect that
someone else can be Christian for us. Let me repeat
Jesus' words:

*If you (not your brother-in-law, or father, or
grandmother, but you) continue (not once were —
but are now) in my word, you will know the truth
and the truth will make you free.*

They answered Jesus, "But we are descendants of
Abraham."

"Where are you with God?" is the issue, and the
people answered Jesus, "But we come from religious
families." Simply being baptized or having your parents,
or wife and kids, who are church members isn't the issue.
"Where am I with Christ?" That is the issue. Simply
being religious or feeling religious or feeling a lump in
my throat on Good Friday or when the flag is marched by
isn't the issue.

Religious-feeling people killed Jesus. Religious
people directed Hitler's war. Religious people killed the
first Christian martyr. Anyone can feel religious from
time to time. Being or feeling religious is not the same as
being Christian. Well-documented social studies now
demonstrate that being religiously active does not in
itself make one Christian in attitude and practice. The
most religiously active in our land are among the most
prejudiced people in our society.

The issue is — *Do you know Jesus Christ — not
know ABOUT him, but KNOW him.* Luther says, "It is
not enough to believe God gave us Christ for our sins. I
must know God gave me Christ for *my* sins.

As your pastor, I'm concerned that some of us are like
"Second Hand Rose of Second Avenue." We inherit a
hand-me-down faith, becoming more concerned with the

form rather than the content, more concerned about preserving old hymns and rituals than working for justice. "No man can die for you. You must stand on the ramparts alone." No man can live for me. I must grab hold of Christ, accept him for myself. *If you continue in my word . . .*

My second pastoral concern centers around Jesus' statement, "You will know the *truth.*" Do we want to know the truth? I suspect we avoid the truth. Jesus says, in John 3, "men of sin prefer the darkness to the light." Like those caught in the probing light of the Watergate investigation trying to cover up, so I find myself at times saying, "Shut off the light." I don't like the truth about me. From time to time, my wife or children will confront me with a truth about myself. I become angry and want to avoid it.

What concerns me is that some of us are prone to say, "I have made up my mind. Don't confuse me with the facts. It doesn't matter what God says to me in the Bible, I have my own opinion." So I ask, to what extent do you allow your mind and life to be controlled by Christ, and to what extent by popular opinions and selfish desire? If Christ is Lord, he must be Lord of every crack, nook, and cranny of our lives. The other day a pastor shared with me a tremendous saying, "Jesus is either Lord of all of your life or not Lord at all." So back to my concern, "Do we want to know the truth?" I suspect that, many times, it's "no." We want God to cure the problems of our lives without having to face the truth and take the medicine. For example, we want inflation ended, but without any sacrifice. The alcoholic wants the hangover and pain of his drinking removed, without removing the drinking. I want peace and harmony on earth, but I still hang on to my little prejudice and shout my racial slur.

There is no cure without the medicine of truth and change. Jesus prescribes the medicine, "Repent and believe." Time and again, day after day, people come to me and want this problem, that painful situation, removed, but without change or reform in their lives.

The marriage has got to get fixed up — but don't expect me to change.

Life doesn't work that way. "Repent, believe, and be saved" is the biblical formula. Unless we allow Jesus to be Lord, let his light to truth shine in all its starkness on our worst and most secret sin, there is no cure. We cannot reserve any little corner of life from him.

This, then, is my second pastoral concern for us. We want Christ to be Savior without being Lord. We want to be cured of our problems and pain and guilt without the light of truth and repentance and change.

The last concern to share with you, " . . . the truth will make you free," says Jesus. Much of our religion is selfish. Our sin is so strong is perverts even our religion. What we need to be free of is our sick self-centeredness; yet, even our religion becomes a private affair between Jesus and me.

I need to be free of the sin of selfishness. The Bible says, "No man can love **God** and ignore the need of his brother." Yet, day after day our Christianity gets reduced to "Jesus and me" relationship and others are ignored.

In a medieval cathedral, an old priest was to have a Vesper service. His sermon was entitled, "Love of God." It was dark when the parishioners huddled in the nave. They were surprised when the old priest came into the chancel with a ladder and a lantern. He placed the ladder alongside of the Crucifix above the altar and climbed to the place where the lantern could shine on the nail print on Jesus' right hand. Then he went to the left. He climbed up the thorn-pierced brow, then down to the spear-wounded side. At each place he allowed the lantern to shine on the wounds of the Lord. The old priest then climbed down to the chancel floor and finally broke the silence with these words, "Can we do any less?" Can we?

Do you, personally, believe, accept Jesus as your Savior?

Do you accept him as our Lord — of all your life — with no reservations?

Will you seek to live and love as he did?

I cannot answer a perfect "YES" to any of these questions. The gospel for me and you is that God gives us his Holy Spirit and we, if willing, can at least make a beginning.

II.
Faith and Conflict With
the Values of Society

THE CHRISTIAN FAITH AND
THE GODS WE WORSHIP

Texts: Deuteronomy 26:5-10
Romans 10:8b-13
Luke 4:1-13

A news correspondent tells the story of coming across a group of natives in an Ethiopian village. The natives had been given an American tractor. As long as the tractor ran, everything was fine. Then, one day the tractor broke down. Being unable to comprehend, because of their limited scientific background and mechanical reasoning, the natives took sticks and beat the tractor as they would an ox in a futile attempt to make it go. Sounds stupid to us. Yet that was a reasonable thing in the minds of these natives. Jesus once said to Peter, "You think as man thinks and not as God thinks!" Again and again Scripture reminds us that the ways of God are not the same as the ways of man. "Man can plan in his mind but the end is in the hands of the Lord." St. Paul bluntly says, "The wisdom of the world is foolishness with God."

The contrast between the Christian faith and the wisdom, the reasoning, of the world is the subject of our meditaton. At times our reasoning must look as foolish to God as the beating of a broken-down tractor appears to us. Yet, we worship reason, especially in America. Reason is one of the major cornerstones of our entire western civilization.

Recently, I had a conversation with several people, and one man commented that he wanted to be a Renaissance Man. He wanted to be well-rounded and fully-educated in the reason and arts of the world. History teaches that our western culture began to really flourish again with the rediscovery of Greek philosophy and reasoning during the Renaissance. Later, the 18th century was called the "Age of Reason," and great leaps were made in scientific and industrial progress. The 19th century was an age of science; the 20th, the age of atomic and space science. We pride ourselves as being "reasonable people." After all, who wants to be unreasonable or irrational? Reason is a virtue in our world. Our whole culture has been shaped by worship of reason. The founding fathers of our country were not Christians, as much as they were Deists, worshipers of a God of reason. A Deist believes in a God who fits his rational philosophy of life. Some have argued that Christianity is the national faith of America. Because of the many people in our country who belong to the church, the many churches, the philosophy and way of life of our country is, *ipso facto* (on the face, automatically), Christian. It is not! Each culture has its own religion. The "American Way of Life" is our cultural religion, and reason is one of our gods.

The contrast between the Christian faith and the cultural religion is not new. The Christian faith, the religion of Scripture, has always been in contrast to and in tension with the cultural religions of the world. The prophets of the Old Testament gave their lives trying to draw the line of distinction between the religion of the God of revelation and the religion of the nations in which they lived. Few listened! Those who did listen were part of the remnant of the faithful. Our own personal concepts of the Christian faith have been distorted and shaped by our culture, by our American cultural religion. The distortion is so subtle that few are aware of the wide contrast between what we think of as Christianity and what Christ actually teaches.

For example:

1. We want a God we can understand, a God who makes sense to us. Man is always tempted to create God in his own image. In the days of old, man-made gods were idols. Today, we are more sophisticated. We make not only physical idols, but philosophical, psychological, and

mental idols as well. We are tempted to say instead, "If God is God, he must end all the war and suffering on this earth, at least for those who believe in him." If life doesn't deal out what we want, then God isn't God anymore and I won't believe in him.

2. Or another way we do it: God must bless our country in a special way. God loves America, or Germany, or Israel, or whatever country we happen to be from, more than he does the other countries. That's only logical. Since I love myself more than I do others, why shouldn't God love me in a special way more than others?

Soon God becomes the God of our country, our society. We use God to bless all kinds of things, groups, clubs, national programs, that we think need blessings. Suddenly, we have a God whom we can manage, a God who will run the world on our terms. If God won't do that, then we stop believing in him. Above all, God must be reasonable enough so I can believe in him. Being reasonable means he will run life the way it makes sense to me.

There is another way we make God and our religion reasonable and fit the rationale of our culture. In our world, the system of most clubs, service groups, scouts, schools, jobs (the whole works), is set up on a "do good and you get rewarded, do evil and you get punished" basis. The harder you work, the more points or dollars you earn, and the higher you climb on the social ladder. So God must work that way also. Thus, the way to salvation is: get baptized, go to Sunday school, get confirmed, cheat as little as possible, be a good citizen, and then you are in with God.

St. Paul says, to these understandings of the Christian faith, *No!* St. Paul says, "I have preached to you not the wisdom of men, for then your faith would rest in man and not in the power of God." Paul tells us the gospel of Jesus Christ is a stumbling block when compared to the reasoning of man. Why? Listen to Paul in Romans

(10:8-13). "Who is a Christian? One who confesses with his heart, not head but heart, Jesus Christ is Lord!"

The reasoning and wisdom of the world says the government, Caesar, is lord. To whom did you give the most last year, IRS or Christ? The reasoning of the world says the almighty dollar is lord. My job, my income, my house, my family, a dozen other loyalties are Christ — lord. There are no rational, reasonable arguments as to why I ought to make Jesus Christ my Lord — except as Luther says, the Holy Spirit has called me, except that I have come to know he loves me more than any other of these earthly lords.

The gospel says Jesus Christ is raised from the dead. There is no scientific or rational proof that ought to force my mind to believe Jesus Christ rose from the dead. Yet, the gospel declares he did. This I cannot believe, unless God has been calling me by the Holy Spirit. The wisdom and reasoning of the world says my salvation is dependent upon me and how hard I work to obey God. Yet, Christ declares that the kingdom of heaven is a gift.

When Jesus was tempted, notice how the devil tried to use reason: "If you are the son of God, then . . . " Jesus was tempted to use the standards of the reasoning of man to measure his life and make his decisions. It is reasonable, by our standards, for Jesus to use his power to turn stones into bread, to feed himself, to gain power over the world. "Just compromise a bit to gain a great goal," so goes the devil's argument. With each temptation, Jesus answered not with the reasoning of man but with the Word of God.

If we ever limit our religion to the reasonable, to the limits of our own mind, we have no God at all. We are then forever earth-bound, grave destined, and will never move beyond our own selfish and distorted view of life. Our reasoning is limited. It is limited to the facts that we can comprehend. It is limited by our own sin. St. Paul says, "claiming to be wise, we become foolish."

In Christ, God reveals to us a way of life that soars above and beyond the limited reasoning we have. It took more than the reasoning, the culture and wisdom of man, to create this world. It is going to take much more than our own power and knowledge to put life back together. Therefore, always check out your faith, your beliefs, your values, your religion, with God's Word.

A beggar, dressed in dirty rags, knocked at the palace gate one day. In the palace lived a king who treasured his pipe organ. The organ had been silent for years. No one knew how to repair it. The king had brought in experts from far and near, and still no one had fixed the organ. So the beggar pleaded with the king for a chance to fix it. Finally, the king said, "I don't see how you can do it any harm." The man worked quietly for days. Finally, he invited the king to hear it bring forth beautiful music again.

"How could you fix it? No one else could," said the king. "That's easy, I was its builder," replied the repairman.

Apart from God, builder and creator, our reasoning is nothing.

FROM TOILDOM TO THE KINGDOM

Texts: Ecclesiastes 1:2, 2:18-26
       Colossians 3:1-11
       Luke 12:13-21

This past week was a hard week! I worked hard all week long. I suppose most of us did. What worthwhile results did all our hard work gain us this week? The Old Testament writer, Ecclesiastes, asks, "I hated all my toil in the sun, seeing that I must leave it to a man who will come after me. He will be master of all I toiled for, and yet he worked for it not. WHAT HAS A MAN FROM ALL THE TOIL AND STRAIN WITH WHICH HE TOILS BENEATH THE SUN?"

That is the Old Testament way of asking, "When you've broken your back and spirit working like a dog all your life in order to build up a big pile, what is it really worth?"

A contemporary popular author or psychologist tells his personal story and asks the same question.

He was thirty-five years old, and an advertising executive. He owned his own business. He thought he had the world's greatest plan for his own life. He was going to work ten to fifteen more years at a business he hated and detested. 'I was going to work a lot harder and faster so I could make a lot of money and I could retire.' Then he suffered a heart attack.

What happened was that his heart said to his head, 'Now look, if you are crazy enough to throw your whole life down a rat hole, chasing something that you don't believe in, that's fine. You can throw your whole life away for money and material gains. But this Norwegian heart, it's not going to go along with you.' While in the hospital recovering from his heart attack he had time to review his life goals. He thought to himself, 'Boy, some way you've gone a long, long way down the wrong path through a whole, long series of rotten, sick, destructive choices. You've gone into things that you've got no sense being in. There is almost nothing left in your life of what you really are.' Then he made a resolution. From this time on, he was never again going to do something that he didn't deeply believe in.*

Here is a man who found new freedom. He found new freedom in God by the decision to no longer sell himself for something in which he did not believe. He was blessed. He took his opportunity to discover that life is more than building bigger and bigger piles of money, and what money can buy. Greed destroys us. The Bible nowhere says, "Money is the root of all evil." It is our *love* of money, the *greed* that focuses our energy and our time in an obsessed way on the making of money, that destroys life. To this, many families can testify after father has made his mint and lost his family or health or life.

I have it on good authority that this letter was actually received by the Internal Revenue Service:

Gentlemen: Five years ago I cheated on my income tax. This has caused me considerable worry and I haven't had a good night's sleep since. I am enclosing twenty-five dollars cash. If I still can't sleep, I'll send the balance.

Love of money has robbed many a man of sleep. We devote a stupid amount of time to making it, counting it, lending it, losing it, spending, banking, investing, and keeping it. Because of our sick, destructive greed for money, Jesus spent more time on the subject of money and property than on most other subjects. Those Christians who want the pastor to stick to the Bible and avoid talking about money and land haven't read the Bible very well.

A young man comes to Jesus and asks him to settle an estate dispute. How many of the families right in our

---

*Paraphrase of Jes Lair's story in *I Ain't Much, Baby/But I Am All I Got*, published by Doubleday and Company.

own congregation have been caught up in the greed of an estate dispute? (Of course, it was the greed of someone else in the family.) Jesus refused to get into the argument of who gets how much. He zeroed into the heart of the issue. GREED. "TAKE HEED, AND BEWARE OF COVETOUSNESS, FOR A MAN'S LIFE DOES NOT CONSIST IN THE ABUNDANCE OF HIS POSSESSIONS."

That is blunt and clear enough. Watch yourself when you get your life fixed on money. Watch those compromises with your time. Watch it when you abandon values (family, church, honesty) to earn a few bucks more. Watch those shady little deals and the wheeling and dealing that locks you onto a course of living for what you can make.

To make the message even clearer, Jesus tells a story. There was a farmer whose land produced great crops. He didn't have big enough barns to store all his goods. So, the farmer decided to expand. He would build bigger barns and make enough money to rest at ease all his life. But, God said to him, "Fool! This night your life is required of you, then what good will the things you have prepared do for you?"

Wow! "What good will a few extra bucks do you when you're dead?" Jesus asks. What good will a few extra bucks do you if you don't enjoy life anyway?

What Jesus is telling us is this: "Leave God out of life, and all you have is threescore and ten years or less, and a desperate squeezing from life its brief satisfaction in terms of eating and drinking."

A poet says it this way:

He always said he would retire
When he had made a million clear,
And so he toiled into the dusk
From day to day, from year to year.
At last he put his ledgers up
And laid his stock reports aside
But when he started out to live,
He found he had already died.

Back to the question, "What has a man from all the toil beneath the sun?" The answer: Nothing that lasts!

If we learn anything from Jesus, it comes in that word *give*. Jesus *gave* his life on the cross in a struggle to free us from our greed. But, greed has such a grasp on us! Let a preacher say the word *give* and we have a ready-built set of defense mechanisms. Eighty percent of the congregation has an automatic reflex action. Hand reaches back to wallet, not to *give* but to protect. And mouth opens, "I'm sorry, I'd like to, but I don't have time to *give*."

Jesus says to you who are afraid to *give*, "Fear not. It is the Father's good pleasure to *give* you the kingdom. . . . God so loved the world that he *gave* his only son."

Jesus says, "Sell all your possessions and *give alms!*" The degree to which you can and do give is a test of your faith. Jesus is not commanding poverty. He is testing you. "For where your treasure is, there will your heart be."

It is one thing to belong to a church, and claim faith. It is another thing to be faithful. It is one thing to try to ride it through on the contributions of little old ladies and widows who, out of their Social Security and little retirement checks far out-give (in percentage and actual dollars) the working folk. It is another thing to risk being generous with our resources. It is one thing to piggyback on the time of others as they organize and teach and call and labor that we might have a church for our families. It is another to pitch in and sacrificially give of our precious time.

LIFE COMES THROUGH GIVING. Mothers *give* birth. We *give* our love. Jesus *gave* his life.

Jesus' challenge — if you want anything that lasts, since you can't take it with you, is this: Can you trust God enough to build your life around *giving* instead of getting and keeping?

Here are two facts about *faith:*

When we trust in God, have faith, we can live in

thanks for whatever we have, rather than in covetous greed for what we don't have. My father was once brought back from death's door when he had suffered a cardiac arrest. It changed him. He said, "Every day is a gift!" Life is a gift. For this we say *thanks!*

The gift of life was meant to be shared, not hoarded. That's *thanksgiving.*

IS CHRISTIANITY A CRUTCH?

Texts: Jeremiah 26:8-15
       Philippians 3:17-4:1
       Luke 13:31-35

Is Christianity a crutch? Christianity has been challenged as being a religion for weaklings. Freud and others have argued that the Christian faith attracts weaklings, people who can't get along in life on their own, so that they want a kindly and healing, fatherly God. A lot of men in our society have this same kind of understanding of the Christian faith. "The Christian faith is for women and kids and old men." This is believed especially by men who have the self-deluding image of themselves as the big, strong, independent, wheeler/dealer businessman, or the rough and ready, outdoor, hard-working, calloused-hands kind of man.

So, the question: "Is Christianity a crutch?" The answer, YES. Yes, Christ is a crutch for weak people. This raises another question, "What's wrong with needing help?" As Christians, we believe there is nothing wrong with needing help. There is nothing wrong in needing God! We believe it is false, and stupid, to think we are so strong and so right and so independent that we become our own little gods and don't need Christ as a crutch.

I'm going to share with you a portion of a letter. It was written by the mother of a little girl who is dying in the hospital.

God knows I'm not alone. There are thousands who are living with a similar nightmare of looking at a beautiful young person prone, a tube in her throat, her right arm stilled by paralysis, the sweet little-girl face once so bright, now immobile.

And the eyes, my God, the eyes. Those pools of

amber sadness that seem to look right through you, then turn away. Will we ever again hear her say, "Mother and Daddy?" Oh, God, what I wouldn't give to hear her say, "Oh, Mother."

What's wrong with being so weakened by illness or tragedy that we need help? You know, it is okay to be comforted. It is okay to need help. Many of us have been raised with such a strong image of standing on our own two feet, of being the comforters, that we don't know how to *be* comforted. We all need help. Even Jesus did. Jesus needed the crutch of prayer. Jesus needed the comfort of friends. Jesus needed the help of the Father.

Some of us have a hard time asking God and our church for help. Let us focus our meditation on some of the psychological, personal, and cultural roadblocks that keep us from turning to Christ for help.

Twelve years ago, a University of Texas graduate student invited my wife and me to a "bull session" group. We were invited because the topic for the night was this proposition: "Christianity is a crutch for the weak." I was especially struck by the innocence and naivete of a young red-haired girl who argued strongly for the idea. She felt it was all right if we were so weak that we needed Christ. But she and her friend were strong enough. They didn't need a God to lean on.

St. Paul speaks about such people. He speaks of "enemies of the cross. People who make their bellies their gods. People who glory in their shame with minds set on earthly things." Paul is speaking about the stupidity of those who think they can "go it through life on their own." Their god is their own belly, their own power. I don't think this girl or this group thought of themselves as "enemies of the cross" or of Jesus Christ. They just didn't need him. So it is with us. Enemies of Christ? No! We just think we don't need him! When I think about that crowd of young people, vital with most of life ahead of them yet, I can't help thinking, but they haven't yet seen life in its fullness! They think they have life by the tail. Who needs God when you are riding high? It's too bad we short-change ourselves, isn't it? We short-change ourselves when we wait until life has us by the tail before we discover we need a crutch. Maybe we aren't so strong after all. We need God.

In addition to being deluded by our own strength, our pride becomes a false god, a roadblock to Christ. I have spoken of "bootstrap religion." By this, I mean the idea that religion is a spiritual welfare office. Who wants to be on welfare? I have pride. I'll make it on my own. Who wants to be humiliated and have to go to the church, to God, to the pastor, to a Christian friend for help?

Before we, like the Pharisees whom Jesus speaks about, use pride as a roadblock to keep us from turning to God for help, we need to hear these words: "self-made," "proud." The first fact I should learn is that my mother went to the gates of death that I might be born. I feed on foods grown by other hands, wear clothes made by other people, use language created by millions before me, have liberty which many a martyr has died to purchase.

We are deluded by our own strength, we stumble over our pride and, perhaps most of all, our sinful stubbornness keeps us from turning to Christ. When God's Word confronts the way we live, our first reaction is hostility! We are more likely to reject, rather than welcome God's Word. Look at Jeremiah and his experience in seeking to get his people to turn from their self-deluding, selfish ways back to God. They took the knife to him and said, "You must die!" Jeremiah was chased out of town because he told the truth. God's Word, God's help, always comes on his terms and not on our terms. So, in our fear of change, out of our own stubbornness, we say, "I'll go it on my own."

It's the old Adam and Eve theme again, "Going My Own Way." We all repeat it, in every generation and in every group. We speak of the dumb, independent Norwegian, the staunch English, the rebellious French, the stubborn German. We joke a little about our stubbornness. We make fun of our resistance to change. So we evade and avoid making any tight commitments to change. Our religion becomes one of our own doing. We have then committed the chief sin. The sin of Adam and Eve. The sin of making our own rules for living, going our own way, regardless.

Stubbornness, pride, delusions about our own strength, one more road block: simply not caring about other people. We are prone to think we are the only ones who count. This is a fourth reason we hesitate accepting God into our lives. I run into this most often in the area of marriage and family problems. One partner will recognize that something is wrong at home. One will pray, ask for help, try one remedy after the other, while the other partner simply ignores the rest of the family and insists, "we can fix life up on our own."

Jesus looks over the people of Jerusalem caught in the delusions of strength, pride, stubbornness and, sometimes, not caring. He weeps! He cries, "How often would I have gathered you together as a hen gathers her little chicks under her wing. But you would not come." God calls us to turn and come to Christ.

One thing I worry about is that, in our religious and church life, we will drink so much coffee and eat so much cake and go to so many church meetings that we will think we have turned to Christ. Instad, we may have simply been churning through perfunctory, superficial activities. Johnny Spence, a well-known professional golfer had become a hopeless alcoholic. He became a ward patient in a psychiatric unit of a government hospital. He tried to commit suicide. Later, the chaplain said to him, "Johnny, all your life God has loved you. You have quit loving him. Not the other way around. You can't do that, son, and live." Finally, Johnny was ready to accept the crutch he needed all along. Life finally started getting put back together again. Johnny was healed when he stopped running from Christ, a crutch in time of need.

Our one desperate need in life is for a new and deeper involvement with God through Jesus Christ. I need a crutch. We need a crutch.

DOES CHRISTIANITY WORK?

Texts: Exodus 3:1-8b-10-15
       1 Corinthians 10:1-13
       Luke 13:1-9

If you received no benefits from Christ, would you continue to love, believe in, and worship him? I'm not sure many of us would answer, "Yes. Yes, I would worship Christ even if Christianity didn't work."

How does God fit into our system and way of life as one who makes things work? We use God as a ceremonial figure. We use Christ as an historical religious symbol. But, how does God fit into our practical working lives? When someone in your family is sick, you go to a doctor. When the physician can do no more, he may pay homage to God and say, "It's all in his hands now." When that is said, do we or should we really expect God to work? When we have economic concerns, we expect Congress to do something. They should do something. When there is war, we look to the United Nations. With phones beside our beds, and phone numbers of physicians, police, and fire departments at hand, we hardly fear the unknown terrors of the night anymore, and so God, as one who wards off the evils of the night, is not often called upon.

"Do we need God?" Let me toss in another serious question. Why believe in a god who does not deliver what we want him to deliver? You would not continue to shop at a store that refused to deliver the goods you wanted. You would not continue to drive an automobile that didn't work.

The central character of John Updike's novel, *Rabbit Run*, muses on the problem of innocent suffering. "Why doesn't God do something? Why doesn't he work?" The husband comes home and goes upstairs. He finds that his

wife, in a drunken stupor, has accidentally allowed their
infant son to drown in the bathtub. The father goes into
the backroom. The water is still in the tub. Some of it has
seeped away. The top of the water is an inch below a
faint gray line on the porcelain, but the tub is still more
than half full. "Stillness makes a dead skin on the water's
now unstirred surface. There is even a kind of dust on it.
He rolls back his sleeve and reaches down and pulls the
plug; the water swings and the drain gasps." The water
slides slowly down the wall of the tub, and then with a
crazed vortical cry the last of it is sucked down. "HE
THINKS HOW EASY IT WAS. YET IN ALL HIS
STRENGTH, GOD DID NOTHING. JUST THAT
LITTLE STOPPER TO LIFE."

I raise the initial question again. "If you received no
benefits from Christ — from God — would you continue
to love, believe in, and worship him?" The question cuts
to the core of our relationship with God.

The questions I have posed are based on the value
system of a religion of pragmatism. The god of
pragmatism is one of the many idols we worship.
Pragmatism is a philosophy and ethic, a religion that
says, "If something works, it's okay. No other questions
are asked. If something does not work, it is to be
discarded and rejected." Pragmatism is a way of life in
which the end justifies the means. It is a way of life that
declares a thing is *good*, if it gets me what I want.
Pragmatism is a way of life that allows our desires and
wants to determine what we will believe is good and
moral and right. There are several different types of
pragmatic religions:

Hedonism — anything that brings me a present or a
future pleasure is good. Anything that will reduce pain
and bring pleasure is good.

There is a second, *utilitarian pragmatism*. This
sounds good, but is again without moral values. Its
slogan is, "The greatest good for the greatest number."
Sound good? You bet! It is a system in which majority

makes right. This kind of religious philosophy was used to justify the crucifixion of Jesus. "It is better that one man die for the nation." It is the standard the Nazis used to justify the killing of the Jews in World War II. It is the standard most politicians use today.

The hearbeat of pragmatism is, "If it works and gets me what I want, I'll buy it, follow it. No other moral questions asked." This is one of the basic value systems of our society. A sign in a locker room reads, "Winning isn't everything. It's the only thing." Do what you must to get your goal.

A cover of *Time* magazine once illustrated the god of pragmatism in the economic world. The cover article revealed a philosophy that said, in effect, "Do anything, even declare it a success before its release, but sell the new supermovie, *The Great Gatsby.* Some physicians prescribe birth control pills for unmarried teenagers without the knowledge of their parents. No questions are asked, other than whether it achieves the desired goal of no pregnancy. Abortion is sold to our population on the "moral" basis of getting us what we want, or getting rid of what we don't want. No other moral questions asked. Capital punishment is being resold on the argument, even though totally undocumented, that it works in reducing crime. It gives the people a sense of vengeance. No other religious, moral, or spiritual questions are asked. It gives us what we want.

The ultimate result of pragmatic religion is a growing web of suffocating moral, spiritual, economic, and political chaos. We no longer are challenged to ask, "What is right?" Pragmatism does not consider anything right or good from a perspective beyond our own desires. The ultimate result is Sodom and Gomorrah, a society bent on its own self-annihilation.

The Bible speaks to us in this kind of religious climate. The Christian faith is not based on man's perception of what works and what is good, but on God's vision of life. God does not begin the Ten Commandments, which spell out our relationship to him and our neighbor, with something like: "Please believe in me, because if you do, you will be happy, healthy, and wise." Rather, God begins with an announcement of his presence. The mystery of our very existence is bound up in him. It is true that life does have more meaning and purpose when we have a right relationship with God. But our motive for faith cannot be and is not because it benefits us. The motive for faith is the fact that God is!

When Moses accepted God's call to go to free the Israelites from bondage in Egypt, that was not the practical or pragmatic thing to do. If Moses' religion had been based on what was best for him alone, he would have spent the rest of his life herding sheep and raising kids! He would have "played it cool" and inherited Jethro's, his father-in-law's, farm. Instead, Moses answered God's call. He risked himself to alleviate the suffering of the Israelites. Moses placed God's will above his own pragmatic desires.

Believing in God, being a member of the church, being baptized, and taking communion does not make us immune from the evil of the world. Jesus is asked why these people are suffering. Is it because of their sins? Jesus refuses to make a causative direct connection between faith and suffering. Life is more complex than that. He answers, *No!* St. Paul warns, don't think because you are a church member you have some kind of eternal insturance policy that protects you from any harm. Not so!

Rather, the Christian faith is a call to the Cross. Jesus said, "Any man who will save his own life for his own sake, will lose it. Take up your cross and follow me." That doesn't sound like a religion I ought to follow simply because it works, because it will give me the best deal! I do happen to believe that Christ gives me the best there is, the forgiveness of sins and eternal life. But, there is more to it than that!

We are called to produce, to work. Christ declares we

are not the judge of the effectiveness of God. We are not the ones to judge God. "Does he, or does he not, deliver life on our terms?" Who do we think we are? God? No, God is God. God is the judge. Jesus told a parable. A man had a fig tree. He said to the vine dresser, "Look, three years I have had this tree. It produces no fruit. Cut it down!" The vine dresser said, "No, let it alone. Give it one more year. If it bears fruit, well and good. If not, you can cut it down."

The ultimate question of life is not: Is God delivering, working for me, giving me what I want? The ultimate question is: Am I working, delivering, bearing fruit for him?

NO PHONY BALONEY

Texts: Deuteronomy 32:36-39
       Philippians 2:5-11
       Luke 19:28-40

I spent Christmas afternoon, 1961, in the cavernous and cold vaults of the Cook County Morgue in Chicago. A member of the congregation had been missing for several days. He had gone out to make some last minute Christmas Eve purchases, and had not returned home. He was found lying face down in a snow bank at the edge of a busy street. I identified his body Christmas afternoon.

The next Sunday in church, several people told me they remembered seeing a man who had passed out and fallen into a snow bank. They thought he was drunk. They walked right on by. He had had a heart attack. No one stopped. No one got involved. He died. He could have been saved, if any one of those people who had passed by had stopped and risked getting involved. What was especially disturbing to the several church members who passed by was that they had sat in church Christmas Eve while this man lay dying in a snow bank. They sat there thinking, and singing how wonderful it is that God loves us enough to stoop down, to risk, to send his Son Jesus Christ to us who need him.

Religious sentimentality is sweet and smooth and goes down easily. But, translating our talk of love into loving action is sometimes bitter and rough and risky. Several months ago, I asked one of our new members why he joined St. Paul's Lutheran Church. The answer I got flattered me and you. The answer was meant to be a compliment to us. "I joined this congregation because it's not dishing out any phony baloney." I appreciate the compliment. I wish it were true. I wish it could be true.

But, my suspicions are that few of us can or do live up to our religious talk. Talk and hopes and dreams are cheap. Action is expensive.

I strongly suspect that I would fit in very well with the first Palm Sunday and Holy Week crowds, singing the sweet praises, shouting the choruses and chants, "Blessed is he who comes in the name of the Lord. Hosanna to the Lord in the highest!" As Holy Week moves on, Jesus translates religious ideals into realities. He begins by revealing the phony baloney, sweet religious talk, for profit of the church. Jesus cuts the frosting off the sweet prayers for the poor, while money was spent on elaborate temples of pagan praise. The church had simply become one more institution in the town, out for a profit. You don't rock the boat. You don't disturb the profit-making systems of high interest and low service. But Jesus cleans out the temple, he tips over the tables of the money changers. He chases the cheap cheats out.

Then, the mob turns. The holy "Hosannas" become hollow. Jesus then challenges the political establishment and reminds the rulers they have no power, except as God gives it to them. The mob is then stirred, and the choruses become curses, "Crucify Him! Crucify Him! Give us Barabbas!" Jesus was a safe and beautiful religious man until he got specific. He was a hero, as long as he spoke in nice "spiritual" generalities.

Palm Sunday starting with its phony cheers and ending with Good Friday jeers reminds me of several lines from a book, *How to Become a Bishop Without Being Religious*. The writer advises pastors, "Your people will be pleased with sermons and religion that help solve personal and spiritual problems as long as you don't ask them:

    a. to stop doing what they like:

    b. to spend any money;

    c. to submit to a rigorous, time-consuming spiritual discipline.

Above all, you don't have to be religious to succeed in the ministry. You just have to look that way."* Jesus dished out no such phony baloney!

The contrast between Jesus and his disciples is vivid. Peter will be Peter the great! He will never deny! But, when "the rubber hits the road," Peter the great becomes Peter the coward, and flees into the dark of the crowded night. The contrast between the great religious words, the cheap chants of the crowds on a spiritual joy ride, and Jesus, is stark.

Jesus began his ministry: "I have come to be with the poor, to deliver the captive, to set free the prisoned, to heal the wounded." That was great religious talk! The crowds were pleased! But Jesus didn't just talk that way. He lived that way. There were the Samaritans, the adulterers, the tax collectors, the sick, the prostitutes, the winos. He was not too good for them. He lived with them.

Jesus talked about forgiveness. That was great! Peter wanted to know, if he forgave a brother seven times, wasn't that more than enough? Jesus said, "No, seventy times seven." Jesus didn't just preach forgiveness, he lived it on the Cross as he prayed, "Father, forgive them!"

What would it mean for us to follow Jesus, to move out beyond phony baloney? First, it means we must let our values, what we love most in life, what we use as our standards for judgment of right and wrong, be set not by our general culture, but by Scripture.

Some time ago, an Omaha paper carried the report of an investigation of American Christian congregations by a study group from around the world. Their conclusion was that we have the most efficient churches and congregations in the world, but — "You are in danger of becoming a state church. Christianity and Americanism are confused as being the same. You are becoming

*Charles Merrill Smith, *How to Become a Bishop Without Being Religious*, ©   , Doubleday and Company. Used with permission.

captive to your own culture."

Scripture says, "Be not conformed to the world, but be transformed by the renewing of your minds." Yet, I would suspect that for many of us we fear nothing more than to take an opinion that stands out clearly from the popular mood. "Be not conformed!"

Second, it means to get involved. Who is to be our model of life if it is not the successful man of our culture? It is to be Jesus. "Have this mind among yourselves which you have in Jesus Christ." Jesus was not afraid to get deeply involved.

We were eating supper Thursday evening. The phone rang. It was a little girl, tragically alone and sad. She asked, "What would you do if nobody liked you?" I can't share the details of this story with you, but it was clear that sweet talk would not help this little girl. She needed not just words of love. She needed an arm of love to reach around her. So we decided to volunteer to work with the school system and with several members of our congregation to reach out and give love to this little girl. We had to get involved with her life.

To follow Jesus means to translate loving words into loving action. That means taking risks. Recently, I spent a day consulting with the directors of Tabitha Home for the Aged. Here are a group of Christians who have real concerns for housing for the aged. They have risked over a million dollars putting together the start of a whole new town for the elderly, a community built to minister to the lonely aging of our society. They took some risks to get beyond the "phony baloney" of religious talk, to action.

It costs to follow Jesus. It is not enough to say that Jesus is Lord and we love our neighbors, and pray for the poor, the sick, the emotionally disturbed, then put a few bucks in the offering plate and try to tip our way into heaven. It's not enough to get upset and complain about lack of adequate medical facilities and a health care system for the poor. To follow Jesus means we put our lives on the line to get involved in changing things in our own community. It means "we put our money where our mouth is" when it comes to taking care of the less fortunate.

Simply to follow Jesus means just what he said. "Any man who would come after me must take up my cross and follow." There is an old religious saying, "No cross, no crown." That makes nice religious rhetoric. It is a true statement. We must be willing to suffer to follow Jesus. But, I find it easier to dish out phony baloney, than to follow. I don't believe I'm yet spiritually mature enough to really put all my actions where my mouth is. I'm not yet strong enough in faith to really risk too much of myself, of our congregation. I'm too practical to follow Jesus to the cross. I suspect that I have a lot of company here this morning. We need to pray, "God be merciful to us sinners." It is easy to chant, "Blessed is he who comes in the name of the Lord." It is hard to follow. As we pray for forgiveness for our weakness, let's try to support each other, so we will gain courage to give more of ourselves in following Jesus. We really need that.

Dear Father: The Cross of your Son occupies a central point in most of our church buildings. Grant that our lives may be as Christ-like as our architecture.

CHRISTIANS TAKE HEAT

Texts: Jeremiah 23:23-29
      Hebrews 11:1-12
      Luke 12:49-53

At the top of Mt. Evans, one of the highest climbable peaks in the Colorado Rockies is a sign: *DANGER: Anyone standing at this peak is a perfect target for frequent lightning strikes.*

Any time we take a moral or spiritual stand that is higher or different from that of the worldly crowd, we stand out. We are then likely targets for all those who like to take easy potshots.

President Gerald Ford, early in his administration, showed himself as a man who at times is willing to stand on the highest moral peaks and risk the lightning strikes. His stand on amnesty before the Veterans Convention in Chicago set him at odds with the popular view of vengeance and punishment. His stand in favor of the small African territory of Namibia, and against the persecution of a minority people by the large and wealthy economic interest of American oil and mining companies and banking interests, again placed him far out front as a target for lightning.

Remember Harry Truman's now famous retort, "If you can't take the heat, get out of the kitchen!" He recognized, as does every human being who has the faith and courage to take a position of moral and spiritual leadership, that you had better be ready to face the flack, the heat of opposition, the lightning strikes of the hatred and rejection of others around you.

So, Jesus warns us, as his disciples. If we are to be his followers, we must not expect the world to love us. The Lord said: "I came to cast fire upon the earth. Do you think I have come to give peace on earth? No, I tell you, but rather division." In another Gospel, Jesus says, "I come to bring a sword and not peace." We don't usually hear these words of Jesus. The more popular words are "Blessed are the peacemakers, the humble and the meek." The usual images and pictures of Jesus are as the man with the children, gentle and peaceful. But here we have the words of Jesus as the man of God, facing a bloody death on the cross, facing the heat and hatred of the world because he had the courage of faith to take moral and spiritual stands which were unpopular. I suspect we so reject and fear conflict that we shy away from this Bible passage. Not many sermons are preached on these words of Jesus. Very few theologians have studied or written on them.

For, here is the Jesus who brings conflict even within the family. Mother and son, father and daughter, husband and wife, are set against each other, if one accepts Christ and the other does not. This does not fit the popular Norman Rockwell image of the Thanksgiving family at table, all heads bowed. Instead we see one member in a deep spiritual conflict with the other, because of Jesus Christ.

How do we deal with conflict caused by our faith? One of the marks or characteristics of the church since the time of the prophets has been suffering. Jesus suffered on the cross. He speaks of his death as a baptism not with peaceful water, but with the terrible painful death of agony on the cross, while all the world rejected him.

Martin Luther said, "You are to understand, if you are a Christian, that you must experience all kinds of opposition." You recall the words of Luther, as all the political and ecclesiastical power on the face of the earth was focused against him. He made his confession: "Here I stand."

Jesus warns us. If we accept him, we must not expect popularity. In the words of the popular song, "I never promised you a rose garden." When you accept Jesus Christ, there is a division between you and the non-

Christian. Kagawa, the famous Japanese Christian, tells of his conversion to Christ at age fifteen. He said at first he tried to have the best of two worlds, the world of traditional Japanese Buddhist society and that of Christ. "I said my prayers at night, under the covers, and then in the morning I would bow with my family to the Buddha shrine." He soon discovered that it did not work. If we are going to be committed Christians, we are going to be in the minority. There will be a marked difference between us and the casual religionist who accepts the trappings of the faith without Jesus Christ.

When you accept Jesus Christ — that must be your own personal decision. When Jesus said, "The house will be divided, two against three, father against son, son against father." What Jesus is telling us is that nobody can believe for you. No one can be baptized for you. No one can receive communion for you. No one can confess your sins for you. Before God, you are on your own. That sounds simple and obvious enough. Yet, we forget and let the wife do the church-going for us. Parents send the children to Sunday Church School while they stay behind. The old-time evangelist, Billy Sunday, said, "You must be more than an in-law of the Lord." Your relative's faith won't save you.

There are some who think that just being a part of our society is faith enough: "After all we are a Christian nation." We have churches on every corner. We have religious rituals as part of every important national occasion. But, we forget there is no such thing as a Christian nation. Only individuals can be followers of Christ! Jesus Christ calls for the division of the house. Where are you with him?

When we accept Jesus Christ, we accept moral and spiritual standards that are not popular, but are at opposition with the world. I wonder about this one. Is it possible that, in our fear of taking an unpopular stand on significant moral issues, be it the former Viet Nam conflict, amnesty, abortion, sexual behavior. honesty in business, impeachment — you name it, that we have become so weak in our faith that our Christianity has lost its bite, so milk-toastish that it simply offends no one? Have we become camouflaged Christians, blending in with the immoral landscape?

I know for a fact that the pastors who are most popular with their congregations are those who take few and weak moral and political and social stands on issues. They offend no one. Is this also true of us as individuals? I think back to Jesus Christ, and the early biblical church. Christianity began as a religion of special appeal to the poor and outcast. Compassion, lovingkindness, was the mark of a Christian. One who took heat for the sake of the minority. Tertullian, an early Christian historian wrote, "It is our care for the helpless, our practice of lovingkindness, that brands us in the eyes of our opponents."

Coretta King said of her late husband, "My husband healed more broken souls and bodies with his direct fighting message than thousands of his colleagues have accomplished with their pallid sermons addressed to half-empty pews. Jesus preached in the street to the poor. He did not timidly and ambiguously imply brotherhood of man. He proclaimed it. He did not mildly disapprove of war. He blessed the peacemakers. He did not worry about popularity with the rich and powerful. He scourned them for their indifference and greed."

How about us and our church? Do we, individually and as a congregation, have the courage of faith to stand up for the right, even when it is unpopular? Do we have the courage of faith to risk doing something for the poor, the economically oppressed, be they young, old, white, yellow, or black? Or, are we so much a part of the majority that we blend right into the landscape and take no stand at all? There is always the temptation to settle for a cheap religion, to reduce stewardship to what we can afford, to baptize and marry without calling people to the discipline of living the Christian life.

I want to close with the words of Dietrich Bonhoeffer, a man who gave his life for his faith in World War II. These are good words to remember as you come to the altar to receive the *blood* (not water), *blood of Christ.*

"Are you worried because you find it so hard to believe? No one should be surprised at the difficulty of faith, if there is some part of his life where he is consciously resisting or disobeying the commandment of Jesus. Is there some part of your life which you are refusing to surrender, some sinful passion, some hate, some hope, some ambition? If so, you must not be surprised that you have not received the Holy Spirit, that prayer and faith remain unanswered. Go be reconciled with your brother, go renounce that sin, and you will recover your faith. How can you hope to enter into communion with him when at some point in your life you are running away from him?" (From *Cost of Discipleship*)

To know the peace of Christ we must decide to accept him as our Lord. Accepting Jesus as our Lord will place us on the cross. The Lord said, "I come to cast fire upon the earth."

III.
Faith and Crisis

NEVER FORGOTTEN

Texts: Isaiah 26:1-4, 8-9, 12-13, 19-21
       Revelation 21:9-11, 22-27
       Matthew 5:1-12

When a new baby is born to a member of our congregation, we now share with them a little card. On the cover is a photo of one little child. Inside is a message, and one line of that message reads, "God calls us by an individual name to be his own and to live in his strength and support." God calls me by name. I'm precious in his sight, just like one new little child is precious and treasured by his or her family.

A teacher asks her class, "What is in the world today that wasn't here one hundred years ago?" "Me!" exclaimed a small boy in the first row. The little boy was right. We come into this world one by one. We are each precious, significant, important in God's sight. The poet T. S. Eliot has one of his characters say,

> Of course, there's something in us, in all of us,
> which isn't just heredity, but something unique.
> something we have been from eternity.
> Something . . . straight from God.*

I'm precious, significant in God's eyes, because he has made me in his image — God and me — we are connected together.

This is what the Bible tells me. This is what my baptism tells me. I have been baptized by name, using my own name and connecting that name with God the Father, Son, and Holy Spirit. "I baptize you, Dennis Anderson (put in your own name) in the name of God the Father, Son, and Holy Spirit." Jesus tells me, in spite of all the millions of people, I'm important to him.

*T. S. Eliot, The Confidential Clerk, ©   , Harcourt, Brace, Jovanovich, Inc. Used by permission.

"Not a sparrow falls to the ground, not a hair from a head, except the Lord knows." "The Good Shepherd leaves the ninety-nine and goes after the one that is lost, and searches until he is found."

If you live to be seventy years of age, the ten billion nerve cells of your brain could help you remember sixteen trillion things, if you could remember them! As Emerson walked by an open casket, he gazed into the face of a lifelong friend and said, "He was a lovely soul, but I forgot his name."

Today is All Saints' Sunday. We are reminded, even though our memories fail us, that we are born precious individuals in God's sight. He never forgets us, though we live or die. Not one human is ever lost in the mass of humanity.

It does seem, though, doesn't it, that God does forget us? I know of the heartache of some of you. We look beyond our own tears and troubles and think of the children with extended bellies dying of starvation, or slaughtered by bombs of war, or dying inch by inch of some unconquered disease. The sparrows do fall to the ground. Sometimes, it seems that God forgets us.

And then I hear Jesus speak, as he does to his disciples in the Sermon on the Mountain. It doesn't sound as if he is promising a rose garden on earth to those who will be his saints. He talks of the poor in spirit — the depressed, those are the ones of whom he speaks. The depressed and down, he says, will be blessed, made happy, for they will gain the kingdom of Heaven because they know they cannot ever be good enough on their own. They are dependent upon God's Spirit. Jesus says that God has not forgotten. There is a blessing even in despair; it can bring us to know we need God in a way the arrogant and proud will never realize.

"Blessed are those who mourn." Jesus speaks to those whose nerves are sensitive to the hurts and wounds of others. You who feel with other human beings are already more human, more perfect, more complete than the calloused and hard of heart. God has not forgotten. There is a hidden justice, even in suffering.

"Blessed are those who are persecuted for righteousness' sake, for theirs is the kingdom of heaven." Jesus speaks to those who are courageous enough to stand for the right when the crowd is pushing for the wrong. Single-mindedness in loving God is the only strength for standing up for what is right when the rest of the world tugs at us trying to pull us into sexual immorality, or lying, or underhanded deals, or malicious gossip, or forsaking our Christian beliefs. Happy, despite being laughed at or considered weak, is the Christian who sticks by his beliefs in the face of temptations and rejections.

Jesus tells us we are not forgotten, even though the blessing is sometimes hidden. But we may forget God and weaken. Will God remember me when I have forgotten him? "This is my body given, my blood shed for you. Do this often in remembrance of me." Even when I forget, God is at work inviting me back to remembering him. I'm so precious in his sight and remembrance that he calls me to be the light of the world. That is what it means to be a saint, a person through whom the light of God shines.

A Christian went next door to his ailing neighbor to tell him of Jesus Christ. The sick man asked, "Do you really believe in judgment, Hell, Heaven and Jesus Christ?" "Yes, I would like to share with you my belief and for you to become a Christian before you die." Again the man asked, "Do you really believe?" When the Christian assured his unsaved friend that he did, the dying neighbor said, "You are a liar! If you believed these things you would have come sooner to tell me about your Savior. We have been neighbors for twenty years."

To be a saint is not to be a perfect Christian, but it is to know, even though I may be cracked and shadowed and not a very good or perfect reflector of God's light, he remembers me and is counting on me.

God remembers me, I'm precious in his sight. Yet, like the sparrow that falls to the ground, so will I. I will fall to the ground and into the ground. Dust to dust.

We nod and admit, "Death must have his day." But, do we give sufficient credit to death's ambition? Death wants not merely one day out of my life. Death wants my life, my breath, my bone, my blood. Death wants darkness now and forevermore.

Where is God's remembrance of me, a precious person in the face of death? Job, in the Old Testament, takes a rather bitter view.

Man that is born of a woman is of few days, and full of trouble. He comes forth like a flower, and withers. He flees like a shadow and continues not. (14:1-2)

But, because Jesus died and rose again, we can say to ourselves and those growing up, and growing old, and dying, that God has not forgotten. Death is not the end. We are so precious and important to God, he will not let Death finish our unfinished lives.

St. Paul says, "Do not be ignorant about those who sleep in Christ. We believe that Jesus died and rose again, and so it will be for those who die as Christians. God will bring them to life with Jesus. At the second coming, first the Christian dead will rise, then we who are left will join them. Thus we shall always be with the Lord." (1 Thessalonians 4:13 ff)

So All Saints' Day reminds us that none of us, living or dead in Christ, is ever forgotten. We are so precious in God's sight! He is at work here calling us. He has prepared ahead, beyond for us. Of what nature is the Beyond? Who knows? The Bible is full of exotic and ecstatic visions trying to portray the nature of Heaven for us. For me, it is beyond my imagination, so, too, for Paul. We can dream and speculate on life after death and what Heaven is like, but our dreaming cannot compare to what God has preapred for us. This, the Bible makes clear.

The great assurance today is that you are precious and so are your loved ones who live and die in Christ. God does not forget us!

How do we know? Listen to these words spoken as the sign of the Cross was placed on your head at baptism: "Receive the sign of the Holy Cross, in token that henceforth thou shalt know the Lord, the power of his Resurrection, and fellowship of his sufferings."

GNAWING GUILT/LIBERATING LOVE

Texts: Joel 2:12-19
2 Corinthians 5:20b-6:2
Matthew 6:1-6, 16-18, (19-21)

It was Christmas Eve. The family was ready to sit down for the evening meal. A visiting relative wanted to take a family photo. The father, a good-looking mother, and two handsome, strong boys, both university students, were seated at the table. A third son, twenty years old and retarded, was over in the corner playing with his toys. The camera was about to be clicked, but the father said, "Wait a moment until I get John ready for the picture." He took the retarded boy and placed him at the table so that he was in the center of the picture. "Now you can take the photo," said the father.

Fatherly love. Not a single child was to be missing from the picture. It made no difference how capable any member of the family was. They all belonged.

That's the way it was in my home. No matter how bad or how many mistakes I made, I knew I would be accepted back as a member of the family. You would never be an outcast unless you counted yourself out.

Now, because Jesus shows us that this is also the way God feels about us, we dare talk about our subject, *Guilt*. We are going to talk about our personal guilt before God.

This is Ash Wednesday, the beginning of Lent. This day has traditionally been that day in the history of the church when we focus on the essential problems of man — not just man — but my essential problem.

There is a yawning gap between what God wants me to be and what I am. That gap is caused by my sin. That gap makes me nervous. I feel guilty, anxious, and restless.

Ash Wednesday is named for the fact that, today, we stop our fleeing business and harried hurrying down the corridors of our life to recognize this fact: From ashes to ashes, dust to dust. That's us! From maternity ward to mortuary, that is the course of our lives. That's it. From ashes to ashes. We don't like to face up to our own limitations and shortcomings. There is a gnawing gap between what I know I can and ought to be, and what I am. Consciousness of that gap is what we call guilt.

The Christian psychiatrist, Dr. Carl Menninger has some interesting things to say about guilt. He comments that one of the reasons guilt has such a hold on us is that we have tried to run away from it. We have invented all kinds of psychological and sociological words and rationalizations trying to escape our own personal responsibility for our sin. Guilt has been a "no-no" in the past few years. We have been told that we are not supposed to feel guilty. (Some people even feel guilty about feeling good.) Guilt has been passed off as caused by a dozen envionmental and sociological-psychological forms other than our own sin. Church is, of course, a place for good people. So, even in church it has not been acceptable to talk much about guilt. We have nervous problems instead. In fact, these nervous problems become quite serious and require hospitalization for physical or emotional symptoms. Dr. Hobart Mower reports a National Mental Health study which indicates that we have been so taught to deny and run away from facing up to our own guilt that only one-fourth of those persons who eventually end up hospitalized because of emotional disturbance will accept any personal responsibility for their problems.

But gnawing away, all the while, has been a host of guilts. We have been substituting depression, anxiety, psychosis, all these other words, for sin and its resulting guilt. Dr. Karen Horney, a psychiatrist, describes three ways of trying to solve any problem. You can move against it, normally called *becoming rebellious*. You can move away from it, normally called *running away*, covering it up. The third, a healthy way, you can *move toward it.* In the church, we'd call the third way *confession.*

Jesus and the Scriptures condemn hypocrisy so strongly, not because that is the wost sin any of us can commit, but because that sin, unlike other sins such as murder, stealing, or lying, is a method of running away, a method of dealing with sin which prevents a solution. Jesus says, "beware of practicing your piety before men" as a cover-up. In 1 John, we read, "If we say we have no sin, we deceive ourselves, but if we confess our sins God is faithful and just and will forgive us." We do feel guilty, every single one of us.

We use all manner and means to cover our guilt. We become pretenders. I'm afraid we all are convicted of practicing a "watergate," a cover-up, a piety before our neighbors, so they won't know how great is the gap and how large is our guilt. The tragedy is that we do this even in church, I suspect most often in church. We cover up and as a result we shut off any chance of God and our neighbors ever helping us. At any given time, there are going to be a significant number in our congregation with marital problems, alcohol problems, children problems, occupational problems. By covering up, even to ourselves, we shut off any chance of receiving help. The yawning, gnawing gap of guilt remains. Instead of seeing and feeling guilt as a fault to be covered, we should feel it as an alarm system calling us to get things straightened out. Luther speaks of guilt as a power that can drive us to God.

There are no short-cuts out of guilt and back to God. Sometimes we have been tempted to short-cut and misuse forgiveness. "Oh, God will forgive us, Jesus loves us, everything will be okay." We hear the message and go away, and wonder why it doesn't take hold, why we still feel guilty.

Traditionally, the church has spoken of three steps to reconciliation with God, to overcoming guilt. Forgiveness is not the end but rather the condition which makes the process of reconciliation possible. Because we know we have a forgiving God who wants us to be a part of the family, we dare to begin. The first step is *repentance*. The opposite of repentance is what the Bible calls "hardness of heart." Repentance is the deep desire to change. Alcoholics, for example, will for years begrudge the morning-after hangovers, the headaches, and the family turmoil that result from their drinking. But, true healing and restoration will not come until they want to be rid of the sin, the drinking, more desperately than they want to be rid of the hangover. Step number one is *repentance*, a deep desire to change, deep enough to be willing to have your whole life rearranged.

The second step is *confession*. The opposite of confession in the Bible is hypocrisy. Confession is facing up to responsibility, a willingness to admit, to share the guilt, to stop covering up and rationalizing away. It means talking to someone about your sin. It hurts to talk about what is real, and serious, and what we have tried to hide. But, as one young girl said, "It was hard, but I guess it was best to get it out in the open."

The third step is to *make satisfaction*. When Zacchaeus was finally made whole, he repaid those he had wronged — and with interest.

In the Absolution we use some Sunday mornings, we are reminded that the Lord gives us "time for amendment of life." If we have really accepted forgiveness, we will want to make restitution to people we have hurt. "A good tree will naturally bear good fruit." It is in the nature of reconciliation to restore the broken, to mend, to heal. Forgiveness is the condition which makes possible the start of a process that ends in healing.

It is my prayer that you will come to know Jesus in such a way that you know that God the Father loves you. That will free you to then dare to take those three hard steps — repentance, confession, satisfaction — and that gnawing guilt will be replaced with a liberating love.

THE FUNERAL OF JESUS/EASTER

Texts: 1 Corinthians 15:1-11
        Luke 24:1-11

We are gathered today to remember a dear friend. We are gathered in this church today for the funeral services of Jesus, son of Mary and Joseph of Nazareth.

Jesus was born in a little town south of Jerusalem, called Bethlehem. Prior to his family's moving back to their home town of Nazareth, they spent some time in Egypt, fleeing from the legal authorities.

In addition to sisters, Jesus had four brothers. He received his early education in the home and in synagogue school. Jesus took his vocational training from his father, and followed Joseph's footsteps as a carpenter. At the age of thirty, he left his father's carpentry shop and became a traveling preacher, supported by those to whom he ministered. Prior to his death, he gathered about him twelve students of the ministry and a large number of would-be followers and admiring crowds.

Jesus was a rather popular man in the communities which he visited. He showed much concern for the ill and poor, and was known as a compassionate man. However, he was often controversial and the talk of the town, because of his rather advanced social theories and his passionate desire to reform both the church and other social institutions. He did not marry and belonged to no social clubs or groups, either in Nazareth or in any of the other communities in which he lived.

Since most of us are familiar with the details of our friend's death, I will only outline the highlights of the *tragic* event. Jesus was tried by both the Jewish and Roman governmental agencies, after being betrayed by a friend. He was found "not guilty of any violations of the law deserving death." However, due to the increasing political pressures brought to bear on the governments of both Jerusalem and Rome, it became expedient to allow the mob to conduct their lynching. He was first tortured and then nailed to a cross along with two other social rejects about 9:00 a.m. He died on Friday afternoon at about 3:00 p.m., after about six hours on the cross. His last words were, "Father, into your hands I commend my spirit."

A secret friend, Joseph of Arimathea, had arranged with Procurator Pontius Pilate for Jesus' body, and buried him in his own tomb. We who have gathered here for the memorial service know that his burial in the tomb is not the end.

We know that, by the power of God, the creating Father, Jesus Christ has been rasied from the dead. So his death, his funeral, is always celebrated and remembered from the joyous viewpoint of his Resurrection!

Imagine for a moment the mood of our service, the vision of life, the feeling about life and death we would have today if the funeral of Jesus had not ended in the Resurrection! If there were no Easter, life would indeed be as the pessimistic poet says, "full of sound and fury and signifying nothing." We would be born. We would live our too-often messed-up lives. We would die. That would be it. Living would be futile.

I once worked as an orderly in a hospital. Late at night a twenty-year-old man was brought to the emergency unit, his skull crushed from a crazy motorcycle accident. He was married. He and his wife and their small child lived at home with his parents. His parents were strong, devout Christians. His young wife had no faith at all. For weeks, he lay in a coma. It was my job to keep him packed in ice to keep his temperature down. We would have prayer together with his parents. His wife would not pray. Inch by inch, he died. Day by day, his wife became more withdrawn and finally collapsed in an emotional breakdown and was hospitalized. The parents, on the other hand, gave thanks to God that, even though they lost their son, he had the promise of Resurrection to life everlasting. For me, this contrast between life and death with and without faith in the Risen Christ is dramatic. The parents and son knew the promise of the Resurrection. The wife had nothing except a short and dead memory.

It is said by Henry Barstow, in a poem:

If Easter Be Not True
Then faith must mount on broken wing;
Then hope no more immortal spring;
If Easter be not true.
What matter though we laugh or cry,
Be good or evil, live or die,
If Easter be not true?*

For many, Easter is not true — it is only a religious holiday. A member of the faculty of the New York Psychoanalytic Institute has written a book entitled, *The Psychiatrist and the Dying Patient.* In it he says, "Belief in life after death has declined to the point that it is of little value to the psychiatrist. Therefore, the need of the dying patient is to be kept unaware of his approaching death. Death is senseless, so is life."

We do try to avoid death. We work hard to avoid death. Some people dream of the immortality of the soul, which they conceive as a mystical part of the body that departs after the body dies, and thus never taste death. This is a delusion of Greek philosophy and not a teaching of the church. It is an attempt to avoid death. "I won't really die, my soul will live forever." Some are even foolish enough to try to weigh the body before and after death, hoping to discover the micromeasure of the weight of the soul. Such dreaming and escaping is foolish, a vain effort to avoid death. Others of us simply try to ignore it.

---

*Henry H. Barstow, "If Easter Be Not True," in *Christ and the Fine Arts,* © 1959, Harper and Brothers. Used with permission.

I don't know how you feel about death. Some of you right now could be saying, "I came to Easter services to hear about living, not dying." But there was no Easter resurrection until after Jesus' death. So for us, our resurrection follows after our death.

Think for a moment about your life. Picture in your mind your own family. Think about your job. Think now about your own death. Let yourself feel it. Think about your family, job, house, after your death. What will it look like, sound like? Think about your funeral service. Now, do you have the assurance that death is not the end? Do you have the personal assurance of the Resurrection? Do you know the reality of the Resurrection for yourself, not just for Jesus long ago on the first Easter, but for yourself? Can you say, with St. Paul, "To live is to be a Christ (servant), to die is gain?" Can you say, "*I* believe in the resurrection of the dead (not immortality of the soul); the resurrection of the body and life everlasting"?

For all our hymn singing and talking about Jesus, resurrection and eternal life, where do I fit into the picture? A survey of our motives for belonging to or coming to church may be troubling. Is it out of conformity, habit, an inherited membership, what a good citizen ought to do? The Christians in the New Testament were Christians because they knew first hand, personally, that they needed a savior to deliver them from the consequences of their sin and from death. We need a savior to deliver us from our sin and death. That savior needs to be something better than simply trying to avoid thinking about death, dreaming of the immortality of the soul, praying for a new medical cure. We need a savior from not just death, but from that which death means. Death means our ultimate failure as human beings. Once death hits me, I am no longer free to change my past, to call back that unkind word I spoke to my wife or children this morning. Death is final. It is the judgment on what I am, because, when I'm dead, I can't fix things up anymore. I am then a prisoner of what I was in life.

I need a word, a sign from God. "My son, your sin is forgiven. My son, Dennis (*put in your own name*), even though you die, yet shall you live. You who are baptized, live and believe in me, you shall be raised unto life everlasting. Because I live, you shall live also."

To hear that word means I must know the Resurrection of Jesus as something more than an event in the Bible. To hear that word addressed to me personally means I must know more than something about Jesus. I must know Jesus. To hear that word means I must inherit more than a church membership, I must receive the Holy Spirit. This promise of forgiveness and resurrection is given to us. When we accept it our lives, yes, even our death, can and will be celebrated like the funeral of Jesus. Like Easter!

LORD, TEACH US TO PRAY

Texts: Genesis 18:20-32
       Colossians 2:6-15
       Luke 11:1-13

A daughter of a neighboring pastor was buried this week. She was seventeen years old. She died after a five-month blood illness. I know many prayers had been offered for her healing, physical healing. She died.

I have stood and prayed with husbands for wives, and wives for husbands, and parents for sick children. Death still conquers. As a pastor, I have prayed for specific persons within our congregation, that they may overcome particular temptations and difficulties, yet they yield. I have prayed and do pray that people will come to faith, and yet many remain unbelieving. The question of unanswered prayer is a serious question, a difficult problem. Does prayer really work? Does it matter that we pray? Or is it a lack of faith when prayer is not answered?

One of our members says, "I'd like to change some bad habits. I pray about these, but always lose my will power. How much will God help me? How much do I have to do to overcome temptation?" Another asks, "How do I pray effectively? How do you know God is listening? Should we even question?"

Let's begin by openly admitting that many of us share in these and other difficulties with prayer. I have my own difficulties with prayer and I am certain many Christians have difficulty establishing a deep and meaningful prayer life.

Some of our difficulties with prayer center around intellectual problems. After all, we live in a scientific age. The Indians may have danced for rain, men of old may have prayed for rain, but we see clouds and develop expensive and extensive irrigation systems. Prayer is reserved for those times when, as Abraham Lincoln said, "I have been driven to my knees by the overwhelming conviction that I had nowhere else to go. My own wisdom, and that of all about me, seemed insufficient." We pray when there seems to be no other source of help. Some of our difficulties center around a feeling that we don't need to pray. Modern man thinks he has outgrown prayer.

A more serious difficulty some of us have with prayer is moral difficulty. We know our guilt, we know our shortcomings, but we really are not ready to lay them before God, and so we avoid him as the kid with cookie crumbs on his mouth avoids seeing his mother.

A third difficulty we have with prayer is a deep spiritual and value problem. Put very simply, "Who has time to pray?" "I'm too busy being active and working toward my success to pray." Now that fact captures ninety percent of the people in any congregation. The news commentator I heard on the radio was right when he said, "The two values we as Americans live by more than any other are: 1) Be active. 2) Be active to be successful." We live in a world of crises and problems that need to be acted upon if we are going to be successful. Fields need to be irrigated. Clients need to be cultivated. Orders need to be filled. Letters need to be typed. We value action that leads toward success more than we value the "inner peace" to which prayer can lead. The forgotten man in our society is not just black or red or middle class over-taxed. The forgotten man is our inner man.

Last Sunday, in the Omaha *World Herald*, there was an article about Marilyn, a young girl dying of cancer. She was noted by family and friends for her inner peace in spite of her oncoming death. She wrote:

> *While an egg whose shell is without flaw seems to be beautiful in itself, it is nothing without the yolk, its inner substance. For without its*

inner substance, it becomes nothing but a hollow shell, devoid of any usefulness, but as a purposeless ornament.

When a person becomes aware of his generous physical, outer attributes, he proceeds to neglect his inner self.

I suggest that one of our most serious difficulties with prayer is that we value outward action and success more than we do the development of what we as persons are on the inside. Perhaps one bit of reassurance with our difficulties with prayer is that they are not new to us. In doing study for this message, I discovered that pastors, for years, have been concerned over their people's weak prayer life. And the disciples asked Jesus, "Lord, teach us to pray." So we join them this morning and make that our request. "Lord, teach us to pray."

Earlier I raised the problem of unanswered prayers, "Does prayer work?" Let me clear away some misconceptions about prayer.

1. I do not believe prayer is a blank check signed by God and handed to us to write in the figures whereby we get anything we want. What kind of father would I be if I granted my children's every whim? Many of the things they ask for are not good. Jesus teaches us that God will give us, not whatever we want, but, *whatever we need.*

2. I do not believe prayer is magic, that if we can say just the right words or pray hard enough, we can make things go our way. I remember being given a Bible once with a brass cover. It was a military Bible, to be carried over the heart. There are many stories of men being saved by a Bible that stopped a bullet. This Bible had extra worth because there was a brass plate as a cover, just in case. Well, that is so much magical nonsense. I do not believe prayer is a bit of magic to ward off trouble.

3. I do not believe prayer is an emergency rip-cord for life, a spare tire to be taken out and dusted off when all else fails.

4. I do not believe prayer is a tool for the religious

professionals only. "Well, pastor, you do the praying for us." I can pray on your behalf, but I cannot pray in place of you.

5. Last, prayer is not some sort of laboratory for testing God. We hear slogans, "Try prayer, it works." Prayer is not some sort of miracle cleanser that works better than anything else. You have heard the saying, "Prayer changes things." No, I don't believe prayer changes things as much as prayer changes people.

Before I can pray with much depth or meaning, I must begin with three basic facts of faith: First, I must believe in God the Father. That sounds simple enough. But, it isn't. When I believe there is a God, then I must have come to that point where I no longer think I'm the center of the world, that all of life must revolve around me and what I want. I submit that much of the time we organize our lives and behave like spoiled little children in a play pen. They scream and holler and fuss and cry and try to force the whole family to center life around them. Their play pen is the center of life. Belief in God is more than saying in my mind, "Oh, yes, someone fantastic out there must have created all this." To believe in God is to know that I'm a sinful person who is going to die, I will not last forever, and I need him. To believe in God is to admit you need him.

Second, in order to pray meaningfully, I must believe God cares. God isn't just some uncaring power or force or flow of ions through eons of time. God is, as Jesus teaches us, "Our Father who art in heaven." Luther says that this means we can come to God in confidence as earthly children come to their fathers.

There is an old preacher's story that illustrates this belief that God cares. A young lad is found standing at the edge of a dock on the Mississippi River. A steamboat is coming upstream and the boy is flagging it down. A stranger comes by and says to the boy, "Hey, kid, you're stupid to think that the steamboat will stop by for you." The lad replies, "No, I'm not. I know it will stop for me."

"What makes you so confident that it will stop for a little boy like you?" asks the stranger. "I know it will stop. My father is the pilot."

God cares and it makes a difference that we pray.

Last: To pray with meaning and depth means we have reached that point where we desire strength to do his will. "Thy will be done on earth as it is in heaven." I believe I can't be like the bride who prayed, "Thy will be done, thy kingdom come, but not until after the wedding." I believe prayer is an attempt to bend God's will toward my will. I believe prayer is not praying just for myself. It is prayer for all mankind, "Give us our daily bread."

Prayer is ultimately an act of submission and obedience to do the Lord's command. Prayer ends in action. Jesus taught us, "Ask, *seek.*"

I suggest that herein lies our greatest difficulty with prayer, with our whole relationship to God. Prayer, Christianity, is ultimately submission to do the will of God. As long as we are trying to use prayer as a technique, worship as a tool for emotional entertainment, religion as a device to get us what we want, we are going to be at odds with God.

For me, prayer is like a wrestling match with God. I usually begin with what I *want.* But, if I'm going to carry the conversation with God to the end, God will give me what I *need.*

Notice that Jesus ends his lesson on prayer with, "How much more will the heavenly Father give the Holy Spirit to those who ask him." What a surprising outcome and answer to prayer! I begin by asking for bread, and God gives me his Holy Spirit, the very presence and power of God himself.

So I ask, "Do I really dare to pray? Am I really ready to live by God's will and in his presence?"

FUNERAL SERMON FOR GARY
[A Young Man Killed In An Accident]

What can we say about today? What words are there that can express the tragedy of this untimely death? No human words can encompass the pain and loneliness, none that can bring comfort and hope and fill up some of the void.

This I know. There are no human words, no neighborly words, no preacher's poetry, that can bring healing and hope. Only God has the Word, the power to bring hope, comfort, healing, when life meets death! When a tragic early death rocks us, as Gary's has, it seems that we are confronted with several ways of responding.

We can and do ask *why?* Why a man so young, so good, so bright, so involved with his community, so strong in his Christian faith? *Why?* It is not fair! Is isn't fair! But, we can get trapped in the search for an answer and miss the Lord's Word to us. It seems to be a chronic characteristic of us that we want to have answers to all things. We seem to need to justify all things. We are tempted in tragedies such as this to settle for too easy an answer. We are tempted, even, to blame God, forgetting that God is not responsible for all things that happen. We are his children, created in his image. We carry both freedom of action and responsibility. Then, there is simple human failure, mechanical failure. The power of evil is still alive in our lives. So, we must take care when we are tempted to settle for too simple an answer by passing to God responsibility for every death, every event in life.

Jesus reminds us that God sends rain to the just and the unjust alike. Our faith in Christ and our moral virtue do not make us immune to evil and death anymore than was Jesus Christ.

God does not will tragedy for his children. Of this I

am sure! The Bible makes clear, beyond doubt, that God gives life. God so loves that he gave his only begotten Son that we who believe might not perish but have everlasting life. God wills us to have life. Death is a part of the created world in which we live. Through sin, death becomes an enemy, not only for us but also for God. The Bible assures us that Christ shall, at the second coming, overcome even the last enemy, death.

We dare not be tempted to pass off responsibility for any or all deaths to God, as do the fatalists, as if we did not have Christ who will overcome death for us.

Even if we had nice neat answers to all our *why* questions, that would not help us now. We need not so much answers to death as we need a cure. For the cure to death, we must turn to God's Word.

A second choice that we have in the face of tragic death is to lose all hope and fall into the pit of despair. The dreams for which we live, and in which we find so much of our hope, are as brittle as delicate glass Christmas tree ornaments, which break at the touch. To find a hope which lasts, we must turn to God's Word.

A third choice is to become bitter and hard of heart. To take this road is to die ourselves. Today there are no human words to meet our need. Let us turn to God's Word.

The first Word from God for us today is in Philippians 3:8-14. This is the passage Gary read from the lectern last winter when he was lay lector.

Indeed I count everything as loss because of the surpassing worth of knowing Christ Jesus my Lord. For his sake I have suffered the loss of all things and count them as refuse, in order that I may gain Christ and be found in him, not having a righteousness of my own, based on law, but that which is through faith in Christ, the righteousness from God that depends on faith; that I may know him and the power of his resurrection, and may share his sufferings, becoming like him in his

death, that if possible I may attain the resurrec-
tion from the dead.

Not that I have already obtained this or am
already perfect; but I press on to make it my
own, because Christ Jesus has made me his own.
Brethren, I do not consider that I have made it on
my own, but one thing I do, forgetting what lies
ahead, I press on toward the goal for the prize of
the upward call of God in Christ Jesus.

Here is the heart, the essence of Christianity. When
we, as sinners, fail, God gives us the perfect gift,
forgiveness. When we, as mortal men, die, God gives us
the perfect promise, *resurrection from the dead.*

I know the promise of the Resurrection does not bring
Gary back to you. The Resurrection is not a substitute
for having Gary now. The Resurrection is God's bold
declaration to us that when evil overcomes us, when
death intrudes upon our life and takes it, God is going to
have the last word. Men thought, when they had killed
Jesus, that that was the end, but God has the last word
— the empty Easter tomb! — the Resurrection, and the
promise "that you who live and believe in me shall share
in the Resurrection."

In one of the great art galleries, there is a painting of
the devil playing chess with a man. The title of the
painting is *Checkmate.* It portrays a devil laughing at the
man whom he has now defeated. One day an old man
entered the hall. He studied the picture and then shouted
"It's not true. The king has another move." Our king has
another move, the Resurrection!

In the second part of the Word from God which Gary
read, St. Paul speaks of, "forgetting what lies behind
and straining forward to what lies ahead, I press on
toward the goal, the prize of the upward call of God in
Christ Jesus."

Our friend and loved one, like St. Paul, looked
forward, not back, up not down, seeking to find the good,
the best, the new, the creative in each situation.

Our faith in Christ does not make us immune to disease, evil, and death. But, God has promised that he can take all things and make them work toward good. Not for everyone, but for those of faith (Romans 8:28). It is hard to find good in a tragedy like this. We can't and won't find it on our own. But, God has promised to work through us, if we let him, even in this hurt, to find good. What are some of the possible blessings we may find?

For me, as a younger man, death like this is a reminder of how fragile is my life. As one of our prayers says, "Lord, make us deeply sensitive to the shortness and uncertainty of human life. Let the Holy Spirit lead us through this life in holiness and righteousness, in communion with Thee and the church, in faith and perfect charity with all mankind."

For me, Gary's death elevates to public consciousness his faith and life. He was a witness! Maybe some of us can learn from him. Gary was a devout Christian. His worship life was as regular as his heart beat.

The Sunday after Gary's death, members shared and recalled his radiant presence in and out of worship. He was a witness! Gary and his wife, both devout Christians of different traditions, showed in a unique way how human traditions can at times be bridged. Gary was concerned for other people and ready and willing to use his talents for the community. This is a witness!

Let no one leave this place and miss the message. I know, I believe, I trust in God's promise not only in the Resurrection for Gary and all who live and believe in Christ, but also that God will work with us, with you, to create some good even out of this, your loss.

IV.
Faith and Our
Relationships

LORD, THIS CHRISTMAS WE NEED
TO BE CLOSE TO YOU

Texts: Malachi 3:1-4
       Philippians 1:3-11
       Luke 3:1-6

One evening during the week before Christmas, several couples were gathered together in Craig and Mary's home for their Bible and sharing group. Craig was a dynamic young man who had gathered the group together as a way to get to know some of their church friends better and to find ways for Christ to become more real to them. After a vigorous Bible and sharing discussion, Craig said, "Now it's time to exchange Christmas gifts." There was an embarrassed silence at first because no one had come prepared to give gifts. No one had brought anything, and no names had been pulled from the hat, so no one was on anyone's Christmas gift list. "How about giving each other gifts that can't be bought at a store. Lets each think of one person to whom we want to give a gift that can't be bought."

Finally, an attorney in the group broke the silence and said, "That's a tough proposition, Craig. A gift that can't be bought? I'm stumped!" Then a Christian psychiatrist in the group began, "Well, this year my wife and I are giving each other a weekend together in the mountains. We need to get away from things. We are going to give each other a weekend of our uninterrupted time. We need to get close to each other and to God again. We need time for each other. So that's what we are giving."

Bob and Lynn were new in the group and they made the next gift. "We promise to pray for every person in the group for the next month." The idea of giving something that couldn't be bought was catching on. Tom struggled with the issue and said, "I'm stuck. I'd like to give to someone, but I honestly am not ready. Perhaps by the first of the year I will be." What he had really given was his own honesty.

Anne, a domineering and self-sufficient woman, said, "I give to my husband the gift of respect. Putting him down, that is what I'm always doing in front of the three children. I want him to know by my change in attitude that he is the head of our marriage and our home."

After everyone in the group had a chance to share his gift, Craig said, "Isn't this what Christmas is all about, this gift-giving business? God so loved that he gave his best, his Son. The best gift we can give is ourselves."

This simple but true incident with a Bible and sharing group shows me what the birth of Jesus is all about. For me, God is only a word. I don't see him. No one has seen him. 'He dwells in light unapproachable," as the Bible says. The word "God" by itself is a strange combination of three letters and simply means someone whom I need but who is too far away to be any good to me now.

But, Christmas tells me that this God loves me enough to give himself, Jesus Christ his Son, in the flesh. In flesh and blood like my flesh and blood. God comes to earth to be touched by people who tried to follow him, but had doubts. And he let them touch him. God comes to earth to be touched by men and women who love him. He washed the feet of his students. He let women brush and oil his hair. This is what Christmas is about, a God who comes to be with us. God does not remain up there or out there as an unembodied spirit ten billion light years beyond the sun.

I have a communion prayer which I frequently use when giving private communion to the sick and home-bound. It says, "Thank you, God, that through this bread and wine — the body and blood of Jesus Christ — you are a God who is not far away, but a God who comes near to be with us, yes, even to live in us."

Christmas, Christianity, is about a God who comes to be in us. The children's favorite Christmas carol, "O,

Little Town of Bethlehem" sings it:
How silently, how silently,
The wonderous Gift is given!
So God imparts to human hearts
The blessings of his Heaven.
No ear may hear his coming,
But in this world of sin,
Where meek souls will receive him, still
The dear Christ enters in.

God comes to be with me. That is the meaning of Christmas. God gives himself to us. But how? I haven't seen Jesus, either. How can we get close to him? He walked this earth two thousand years ago. That sometimes seems just as far away as ten billion light years beyond the sun.

I did not come to know Jesus just by reading a lot of books or studying a lot about him. That is important. But it is more important after you come to know him, than before. I came to know Jesus through other people who knew him. When I look back at my own spiritual pilgrimage, which is still going on and has a long way to go, I was most spiritually awakened when I let other people, in whom the Holy Spirit was alive, get close to me. God comes to us, not as a bolt of spirit in a vacuum from outer space, but God comes to us when we let others who are close to God in Christ get close to us.

We have a hard time doing that though, don't we? We want to keep our religion and our life a secret, personal affair. This whole business of repentance is a good example. When we repent of our sins, we feel most comfortable if we can get in a little quiet place by ourselves and just talk to God. That is good and necessary, but that is not enough. Why? First, because we don't live all by ourselves, we live with others. So, we don't sin all by ourselves. Second, we don't sin in the closet in secret. We sin among other people, and other people bear the hurt of our sin. So our repentance can't be in a vacuum, because we don't live or sin in a vacuum.

That is why God, in the letter of James, urges us, as Christians, to find a brother — some person in whom we have spiritual confidence, and then confess and repent of our sins. Repentance isn't just feeling sorry for what we have done wrong. The word repentance means to make a public change for the better.

I know of no one who has been reconciled or healed of a broken human relationship who avoided this step. We get close to God through people.

A great philosopher, Unamuno, said, "The world needs not just more light, but more warmth. We shall die not from the dark, but from the cold." This is what Christmas and Christianity and knowing Jesus are all about.

Forgiveness involves more than a simple pronouncement that you are not held accountable for your sins. Forgiveness involves a fellowship now. Eternal life is not just "pie in the sky" for tomorrow. It is a present reality. It is a quality of life in Jesus Christ which results in fellowship now, today. God is not a God way out there. He is a God who is here. He gave us himself through Jesus in the flesh. Today he gives us himself through the spirit alive in the flesh of his people.

When we allow God to become close to us, we become closer to other people. St. Paul says today, "Welcome, accept one another as God has accepted you." No man is complete without his neighbor. How can we become a congregation of more alive Christians, closer to each other and to God? I have an idea. Let's try it. Think of one person with whom you have had trouble getting along. Now this week, find a way of getting that straightened out. If we can't do that — let's get at least one human relationship straightened out by giving ourselves to that person. I wonder if Christmas for us isn't reduced to so much sentimental but meaningless "slush." Let's work on that this week.

GOD LOVES SINNERS/
YOU DON'T WASH CLEAN DISHES

Texts: Exodus 32:7-14
1 Timothy 1:12-17
Luke 15:1-10

"Why baptize babies? They haven't done anything wrong."

Compare the moral lives of little infants to that of their parents and they have done nothing more than cry and dirty their diapers, while mom and dad have each done their share — perhaps more — of sinning, cheating or lying, or fudging a little bit here or there. While the infants have done nothing. That's just the point, in part, they have done nothing. Yet, God's love in Christ is still for them. In baptism, we have a perfect example of the gospel. God's adopting love, Christ's accepting love, for those who have done nothing to earn or win it. As one Christian said, "I was baptized at the age of two weeks, before I had any education and while my personality was zero. God accepted me then simply as a human being. Now I don't have to lie awake at night worrying whether I lived acceptably that day, because God still loves me, mistakes and all."

That's what baptism is all about. Jesus Christ, God, loves you, mistakes and all. Jesus came into the world to accept sinners. But wait a minute. Have these little babies sinned? What did they consciously do that was wrong? No, they have not consciously sinned. Yet they, like us, are born with a natural tendency toward selfishness. Anyone who says children do not sin, hasn't been around babies or children much. Sin is simply to organize life around *me*, with me in the center. We all do that, even babies. The tragedy is that we sometimes don't even know we have sinned, as Jesus prays, "Father, forgive them, they know not what they do."

Yes, I know we sin and we don't even know it. As a pastoral counselor, this realization is brought home to me many times. Very few of us are consciously out to hurt someone else. Few of us are psychopathic personalities, consciously evil. But we fall into our own traps. We fudge a little here, cut with our tongues a little there, simply trying to satisfy a basic human need. We end up sinners — sometimes without intending to be evil.

Someone asks, "Are you saved?" The tragedy is that we all, like sheep, have strayed each to his own way. Are you saved? "I didn't know I was lost." Yet there is an uneasiness. Deep down we know all is not right with us.

Baptism is God reminding you, "I still love you, accept you as my child even though you wander away. Come back and live as a child of God." Baptism is a washing. You don't wash clean dishes. Here are some dirty dishes. In water, we wash them clean. But we add something to the water, soap — a solvent. So, to the baptismal water is added God's Word in Christ, his promise of forgiveness — a solvent to our sin. You don't wash clean dishes. God doesn't call perfect people. He has called you. He has washed you clean in baptism.

When this fact dawns on you, there is a conversion in your life. As Lutherans we seldom use this word, conversion. This conversion may be a slow gradual process over the years as imperceptible as the sunflower's turning toward the sun. But, finally, at the dawning, you become aware. Or, it may be a dramatic momentary experience. "Yes, God does love me and that makes a difference."

St. Paul describes this as his experience. "I once blasphemed and persecuted and insulted Christ," he said. This is true of me, of us. We ignore him and his needy children. We sometimes outright reject him. "I won't worship. I won't serve. I won't give. Let them do it themselves." We curse and take his name in vain.

Paul says, "I acted ignorantly because of my unbelief." Which one of us can say we are unlike Paul, acting ignorantly because of unbelief? When this is the case, we need a conversion, an awakening. Robert Mowrer, a Christian psychologist, rightly says that we cannot grow or make a personal change unless we acknowledge our wrong, our sin. Jesus says, "Repent and believe." Jesus makes it possible for us to dare to repent and believe because, instead of smashing us for our wrong, he forgives us. So, Paul confesses, "Jesus came into the world to save sinners. I am the foremost of sinners." I am a sinner. I am a failure as a human being in many ways. The only way I know how to handle this fact in a healthy way is to know, Jesus saves sinners. I have been baptized!

St. Luke tells the dramatic event of salvation in the life of Zacchaeus. He describes how and what happens when we let Christ's acceptance of us take hold.

Jesus comes into Jericho, Zacchaeus' home town. He is surrounded by huge crowds of people eager to see and hear the wonder-working street preacher from Galilee. There is Zacchaeus, a lonely man, short of stature, not only physically but, even in his own eyes, he was short, a small human being. You know how it feels to feel lowly, little. So Zacchaeus spends his life trying to be tall. He gets a rotten reputation in the process. He'd sell out his own mother if it made him feel better, even for a minute. He's not a "jail-bird" type. He is in the upper levels of social power. He has a good government job. But, he is a little man inside. He has built his life on the principles of a "fast buck," whatever makes you feel good, do it. As the bumper sticker says, "If it feels good, do it." But, Zacchaeus is not really much different from many of us. We compromise quite easily with our tongues and our pocketbooks.

But Zacchaeus, like us, is not all that satisfied with himself. He knew inside he was small of stature. So he climbs a tree to see Jesus. Along comes Jesus. And of all people in that crowd of sermon tasters and miracle seekers, Jesus stops to talk to Zacchaeus. "Come down out of that tree. I want to come to your house." The crowd grumbles. Jesus eats and drinks with sinners! He wants to be a guest of sinners! The word *guest* means literally to relieve the burden. Jesus wants to relieve the burden of sinners. I can imagine the dinner conversation. Zacchaeus says, "Jesus, it is not easy being like me. I know I'm not what I ought to be."

Like the frog song on *Sesame Street:*
It's not easy bein' green,
Having to spend each day the color of the leaves;
When I think it would be nicer bein' red or yellow
*   or gold,*
Or something more colorful like that.

It's not easy bein' green
It seems you blend in with so many other ordinary
*   things,*
And people tend to pass you over, 'cause you're
*   not standing out*
Like flashy sparkles on the water or stars in the
*   sky.**

But, Zacchaeus was so moved by Jesus' love that it *changed* his life. Jesus simply accepted Zacchaeus. Zacchaeus was so overcome that he said, "Behold, half of my goods I give to the poor, and if I have cheated anyone I will repay fourfold." "Today," said Jesus, "salvation has come to you."

I can imagine another piece of the conversation between Jesus and Zacchaeus. Jesus asks, "Zacchaeus, what made you want to climb a tree to see me?" "Good master, I saw mirrored in your eyes the face of the Zacchaeus I was meant to be."

In the water and word of Baptism, Jesus calls to you, "Come, I want to come to your house." Do you see in Jesus the "you" God means for you to be? Sometimes I think we are afraid of the change that will happen if we let Jesus in and really take our baptismal sonship

---

* © Copyright 1970 and 1972, Jonico Music, Inc.

seriously. Zacchaeus changed his way of living.

If I accept Jesus' forgiveness, I must let go my little idols and golden calves. Like Zacchaeus, I will have to reorganize my mind, my bank account, my life. In Baptism, we are washed clean, accepted as sons of God.

Let us live, then, as God's children. Not as alley urchins, grabbing and getting, fighting and bullying, scrounging and scraping, hoarding for little pieces of bread as if we had no loving Father, no tomorrow.

WHAT'S THE DIFFERENCE?/
IN THE DIFFERENCE IS HOPE

Texts: Proverbs 25:6-22
        Romans 12:14-21
        Luke 14:1, 7-14

Little Speck was a fish. He spent most of his time under a rock. He was the smallest trout in the brook. He daydreamed about being bigger and stronger and better than all the rest. "Someday I'll show 'em," he thought to himself. But, little Speck was too timid and wouldn't budge from under his rock.

One day, while Speck was hiding in his safe home, a fat, juicy worm squirming on a thin shiny object came to rest in front of his nose. Speck nibbled at the treat and zap! Speck felt a sharp pain in his jaw as he was jerked into the fisherman's boat. "Look at this little fellow," grinned the fat fisherman. "Wow, let's throw a fish fry," said his partner. They roared with laughter. "Wanta use him as bait?" "No, we don't have a hook that small." And the fisherman laughed and threw little Speck back into the water. Speck was so humiliated that he resolved to change. "I'll never be laughed at again. I'll show those fishermen," Speck swore, shaking his fin in anger. From that moment, Speck was a new trout. Speck ate like a piranha. One day he gobbled his first fellow trout. He felt a little squeamish at first. Eating a brother didn't seem right. But Speck remembered the fishermen's laughter. "Heck with it," he mumbled. "Winners don't ask questions." Speck grew bigger and bigger and became the most ferocious fish in the stream. He was the strongest, fastest, biggest.

One day, the fishermen returned. Speck darted through the water. He chomped the bait and heard the fisherman gasp at the sight of him. Speck felt the sharp pain in his jaws. But, he didn't mind. "Winners have to be tough," he said. Finally the fishermen landed Speck. They couldn't believe their eyes. Speck was a once-in-a-lifetime catch. Speck beamed with pride as they measured him, bragged about him. "They're not laughing now," he thought as he lost consciousness. The fishermen took him to the best taxidermist in town and had him mounted on a mahogany plaque. He was then placed over the fireplace with a bronze name plate on which was inscribed *The Winner!* (Story by Wes Seelinger, adapted)

When I read this story, I couldn't help wondering how many people whom our society declares to be *winners* are like Speck. We have bought a way of life, a set of values, and swallowed them "hook, line, and sinker," thinking we were right in there working our way to the top, success, and victory, and all that counts. But, like Speck, we can be *taken* by a false line of life. He accepted the standards of the fishermen as a standard for living. Many of us do likewise.

I find it so easy to want to be a good guy and to be accepted, that I can become, without thinking, a carbon copy of the world around me. Unwittingly, we start thinking, behaving, dressing, enjoying movies, reflecting political opinions, exactly as our associates do. Soon, *their* standards are *our* standards. Their values are our values. We all start thinking and looking alike. "We must be right and those who are different must be wrong."

One of the most upsetting facts about our world right now is that many of us are discovering that we have been like Speck. That we have fallen for a set of values and a life style that we thought made us "winners," but it turned out that we were losers in the long run. Books like *The Greening of America*, popular several years ago, reflect the anxiety that has been raised by the fact we fought the Viet Nam war and half-way through, it became a nightmare of moral terror. Then Watergate, world hunger, recession, a panorama of problems face us

— war, hunger, political stress, corruption in government, crime, and others.

What is right? What is wrong? It seems that the old, simple slogan solutions don't work anymore. This is emotionally disturbing. It is upsetting to have values you once worshiped turn out to be tin gods and rusting cans of materialistic idolatry. Some persons, in their hopelessness, simply are shouting the old pietistic, or nationalistic, or materialistic slogans louder. Others are ready to give up. Where is the hope when all the old lights seem to have been blown out?

As a Christian, I find hope in the fact that some of the old values are blown out by God! As a Christian, I believe that God is active in our lives, turning our tin gods and rusty values upside down. I believe that God is trying to stand us on our heads to shake out the sawdust and set us right side up again. As a Christian, I find *hope* in the new standard for living which Jesus brings. Listen to what he tells. "When you are invited to a dinner, take the lowest seat. Then you who are humble will be exalted, and the exalted will be humbled." Jesus is showing us that the measure of right and wrong which our world teaches is turned right side up in the Kingdom of God.

The standards of the world are at war with the standards of God. You lose hope if you have been banking on the "tin-god" standards of the world. When they rust and fall apart, no wonder you are disturbed. Jesus is here asking us to measure our values. "Dennis Anderson, are you building your life by the social rule book, *Etiquette and Social Ethics of the Grand Island Chapter for the Preservation of Things as They Are*, or by *The Life of God's Servant by Jesus Christ?*"

As I think about that question, I find myself disturbed. What about my life? Is it different because I'm a Christian? The classic question is, "If Christianity were a capital offense, would there be enough evidence to convict you?" What's the difference in the way I live and the way a non-Christian lives?

Our Bible lessons outline at least three differences between one who lives by God's values and one who lives by the values of the world. Here they are:

First: Hurray for the second string! I remember my efforts as a high school sophomore trying to play football, and the agony of being on the second string, warming the bench. The crowds were cheering for those heroes on the field. The shame of having a clean football jersey. Boy, you were not worth much if you were on the second string, not unless all the others failed. You became great only when others failed. Greatness, goodness, value, were not measured by what you were or stood for as a person, but by how much more you could do than someone else. To be first string, some other human being had to lose. In our society, the old and retired are sometimes valued as second string. We pit youth against age. We pit mind against mind, income against income, one side of town against the other side of town, black against white, farmer against town.

Second: Hurray for the second team! God values people by a new and better standard. What is your standard for valuing people? Income, degrees, dress, social status? How are you different from the non-Christian by the way you value life? Jesus says, *Invite the bums in!* The world says, *Throw the bums out.* When we give a banquet or dinner, Jesus reminds us we tend to invite our own kind, those whom we agree with or like, or those who can do us a favor. "You scratch my back, I'll scratch yours." "Why not," he asks, "invite the poor, the maimed, the lame, the blind?" Invite the bums in. In other words, what have you done for those people who can in no way return a favor for you? How are your values, how is your life different from the non-Christian?

Third: "Scrap the Scapegoating." We usually want to find someone to blame for our problems: the Jews, the Communists, the Niggers, the middleman, the — put in your favorite scapegoat. We like to divide life up between good and bad, friend and foe. When anyone does us wrong, "Man, am I going to nail him/her to the wall!" The Lord says, "Repay no one evil. Vengeance is mine." We have a hard time accepting that. Look at our reactions to the questions now before our government. Our anger cries for blood. The Lord cries for mercy. I'll never forget a sermon I heard while a seminary student in Rock Island, Illinois. Saturday night, at a special congregational meeting, the pastor was terribly maligned and attacked by people in the congregation who disagreed with him. He was treated bitterly. But, the next morning he built his sermon on the message we have before us: "If your enemy is hungry, feed him, thirsty, give him drink. For, by doing so, you will heap coals of kindness on his head. Do not be overcome by evil, but overcome evil with good." And he forgave the congregation for their evil.

Scrap the scapegoating, Invite the Bums in, Hurray for the second string — these are new values Jesus teaches.

There is hope in the new order that Jesus brings. People are looking for that new light and new order. All our words to the world will not bring hope. Our living by a new value will. The question is: "If the Lord ordered the churches silent, what would the world hear?" They would hear what we say in our living.

IN THE SPIRIT OF CHRIST

Texts: Acts 8:26-40
       Revelation 1:9-19
       John 20:19-31

The triumphant trumpets are silent this morning. The brilliant banners are back in their storage places this Sunday. Gone, too, are the Easter crowds. Our scene today is not unlike those first days after the Resurrection.

You'd think that, after something as awesome as the Resurrection, Jesus would have run a crusade from the Jerusalem Colosseum that never ended. Ater all, dead men don't rise from the grave. What a tremendous show that would have made! There could have been packed houses day and night. Jesus could have become friends with kings and emperors, or even become a king himself. He would have made any of the crusades of Billy Graham look like Saturday night in Doniphan or Cairo by comparison. But, instead of a dazzling display, he met quietly with his disciples in a closed room. They talked, asked questions, argued a little bit, and then Jesus gave them their life assignment.

The mountaintop experience of Easter is over. But, now Christ has some conversation for those of us who are ready to meet with him at the bottom of the mountain, outside the crusade colosseum, after the glory days are over. We are back to the grubby day-by-day world. Jesus did not seek the crowds after the Resurrection, because we can't be dazzled into believing and living as children of God. After the Resurrection, Jesus quietly met with his disciples and gave them their life assignment. That is what we receive today. The risen Lord holds a meeting with us to give us our living instructions, and our power for carrying out his orders. Here they are:

As the Father has sent me, even so I send you.
Receive the Holy Spirit. If you forgive the sins of
any, they are forgiven. If you retain the sins of
any, they are retained.

There it is. Those are the instructions Jesus gives to us. I'm a little like Thomas when I heard those words. You mean God sends me, expects me, to be a little Jesus? "As the Father sent me so I send you." I gulp a little and swallow kind of hard on that. After all, we have just been through the terror of death on a cross. What assurance is there that we will come out of it alive? With an assignment like that, it is no wonder Jesus did not gather crowds for a crusade in a colosseum!

Thomas comes up with the best possible defense against accepting that kind of assignment. "What proof do you have that Jesus is raised from the dead? You prove beyond a reasonable doubt that he is risen, and I will follow!" Thus, Thomas approaches the Resurrection, the whole issue of following Jesus.

I can feel pretty comfortable with Thomas. If I were there, I strongly suspect I would have cheered Thomas' defense. After all, it is not rational, practical, logical, or scientific to believe in men raised from the dead. "Where is your scientific proof?" You see, if that question is not answered, then I'm "off the hook" and I don't have to follow Jesus, that is, try to be like him.

Our minds have been so trained to believe that scientific proof is the ultimate test of truth, that we are literally imprisoned from two-thirds of creation. Dr. Richard Bube, a professor of science at Stanford University, says, "One of the most pernicious falsehoods ever to be universally accepted is that the scientific method is the only reliable way to truth." Dr. Theodore Roszak says, "Human reason is a limited skill. Only one among many. There is also spiritual knowledge and power."

We could go on discussing the role of science and reason in life for the next two weeks. The point is this:

we can use our questions of doubt or skepticism about Jesus, Resurrection, the Church, etc., as excuses for not following, if we want excuses. All the science in the world will not convince any one to believe in Jesus.

Believing in Christ is not unlike falling in love. Someone has touched your life and your life must change because of that person. It is almost funny when couples come into my office for premarital counseling. There are a number of times when, as an objective bystander, I can see they would be far better off, practically speaking, if they would wait another year to get married. They could then save more money, know each other better, and reduce some of the risks of marriage. But, after experience, I know it is impossible to try to use the logic of economics with a couple deeply in love. They have been touched by each other at a level far deeper than will science, reason, logic, or the future bank balance. They are going to get married! They are going to give their lives to each other! They may not have all the answers worked out. There still are a number of doubts and difficulties, but they have made a commitment to each other. Their faith in each other absorbs and takes the difficulty out of their doubts and even the hurts they will sustain.

Faith in Jesus is like that. It is not a matter of rational mind only, primarily. It is not a matter of following when all the questions are answered. They never will all be answered. *It is a spiritual decision of the will.* It is a commitment I make with my total being. It is a spiritual decision I make about my whole life. Like falling in love, it shows. There is a glow, a change in what and whom we talk about. There is a change in our lives.

When we believe in something, we first talk about it. Second, we live it. These two things happen naturally. First, talking about our faith: there is no substitute for talking about what we believe. The writer of Acts tells of Philip, the evangelist. Philip talked about his faith in Jesus. Instead of being trained to talk about our faith, many of us have been trained to keep quiet. "You don't talk about things that are personal and important!" That is the atmosphere in which some have been brought up. We *so* resent the person who pushes his religion on us, that we overreact and don't say anything.

When someone starts telling me that I should talk about what I believe concerning Jesus, I envision something like this happening. George Brush was an upstanding young man of strong Christian belief. He was a salesman. He talked about his faith to everyone he met. One day he got another businessman in the car and asked, "Brother, may I talk to you about the most important thing in life?" The man looked at him and said, "If it's insurance, I've got it. If it's oil wells, I don't touch them. And if it's religion, I'm saved." That ended the conversation. So, not wanting to be turned off, afraid of offending people in the wrong way, we keep silent. This is no solution.

I have discovered recently that there is no substitute for talking about the person, Jesus. But, you have to wait for the right moment. People are interested in getting their lives straight. We can send them to psychiatrists, doctors, clinics, and schools but, if we keep silent about where they can come to experience love and forgiveness and belonging, we have offended greater by our silence than by the risk of talking about our faith. I have been discovering in my own life that there are times when people simply have to be asked, "Isn't it time you considered this problem of yours in relationship to Jesus Christ?" You know, people seldom turn that off. I'm pleased with the number of people who bring others to worship and study with them.

Second, Jesus says, "Forgive sins." Talking about our faith is not enough. We have to live it. Jesus counts on us to demonstrate his love in action here on earth. No one is going to know the love of Christ, the forgiveness we need, out of the clear blue sky. God's love comes through people. He calls us to be his forgiving people. That means giving to people who may take advantage of us. It means less for ourselves and more for others. It costs to be followers of Jesus. "As the Father has sent me, so I send you."

RESURRECTIONS STILL HAPPEN

Texts: 1 Kings 17:17-24
       Galatians 1:11-24
       Luke 17:11-17

At the bottom of an inside page in the *Grand Island Independent*, there was a two-paragraph report of a tragedy of disillusioned hope and twisted faith. A California couple had taken their seven-year-old son off insulin because he "had been healed" of his diabetic condition at a healing service. He died at home. They refused to bury him. They were waiting for Jesus to bring him back to life.

The Bible has several dramatic stories of healing and of bringing the dead back to life. We have two such events in our lessons. First, Elijah breathes life back into a child. Second, Jesus has compassion on the widow of Nain whose only son died and is being carried to the cemetery. Jesus stops the funeral procession. He says, "Do not weep!" and commands the young man to rise. "And the dead man sat up and began to speak."

Contrast these Bible events with today's events and it would be easy to come to the conclusion: "God brings life to the dead in the Bible. That's good for *back then*, but not for today." How do we interpret these events both in the Bible and today?

Jesus has given us a promise in the Resurrection of the body at the second coming. That promise is for the future. Then he gives us a promise for today. Resurrection from spiritual death now. This promise is being fulfilled now. Let me share with you the story of a young man I met this week.

This young man, let's call him Kurt, saw a key chain I have. That key chain has a cross on it. He asked what church I belong to. I told him, not revealing I was a pastor. I inquired if he were a Christian. His reply was fascinating. "Yes, I'm a new Christian." That phrase, "new Christian," indicated an interesting past. He had been in Viet Nam. He had become a user of drugs, a fairly heavy user. When he came back to his home town in Ohio he met a young girl who introduced him to Jesus. He said, "I was raised in that town. It has fifteen churches and I don't recall any of them introducing me to Jesus. They introduced me to their religion, yes, but not to Jesus. When I met him, it was just like it says in the ·Bible, 'I was in the land of the dead and now I was made alive.' I was really far out — out of touch with reality. It was like walking out of the darkness into light. Everything became real to me." Then he used a phrase we have heard from former drug users who open up to Christ, "Jesus gave me a high, higher than any drug, and better. At first, I got carried away with my new birth. I tried to push Jesus on everyone. Now, I just quietly try and tell and show what he is all about. I was looking for love and peace when I was on drugs. What I got was what too many got — sex and violence. Jesus is love and peace."

When these kinds of events happened in Bible times, people declared, "A great prophet has visited the people." That is what it says in today's texts. We get so mixed up on what a prophet means that we don't understand these events. A prophet is not a fortune teller of the future like Jean Dixon. The word for that kind of occult people in the Bible is soothsayer. No, a prophet is one who introduces people to God, one who speaks forth God's life-giving message. The young girl in this man's life was a prophet; she was the one who introduced him to Jesus. When he met Jesus, he found a new life. This still happens — "the dead are raised" when we meet Jesus.

Jesus grants us freedom from our past through forgiveness. Have you ever had the experience of returning to your home town? It is filled with nostalgia and memories, good and bad. One of the disappointing things about returning to places where we have been is that we discover how hard it is to move away from our past. The mistakes of the past become a part of us and can and do haunt us, follow us wherever we go. So, we raise a very real problem for every human being: "How can I get free of the past?" Must the past determine my life? For everyone of us there is that sin, that past which is unspeakable. It follows us. Psychiatrists affirm what pastors have known for years. Today's marriages are often destroyed by yesterday's sins that haunt and hunt until they are dealt with. The child is the father of the man. Psychiatrist can help us become aware of the fact that we are what we are today, because of what we were yesterday. But how can we become free of the past. A noted English psychiatrist says, "I know of no answer to the question; as a man, I can only say that I believe in God." It is when we meet Jesus and hear him say, "Your sins are forgiven" that we are raised from the dead past and free to be for today. Jesus says to you, "My son, your sins are forgiven. Go and sin no more." So we do have a new life free of our past.

Jesus gives us freedom from bondage of our present weakness. He says, "Unless you are born from above you cannot enter into the kingdom." In Genesis, we are told that we are made of the stuff of the earth and we become living beings only by the breath of God. Without that Holy Spirit, that breath of God, we are bound to the earth.

St. Paul says it this say: "Man is either of the flesh or of the spirit." We become bound not only by our past but by our present weak egos and the habits we develop to protect our weak egos from reality. There are six million alcoholics in the United States. Alcoholism is our largest single mental health problem. There are an estimated seven million compulsive gamblers in the United States. Nicotine is a worldwide way of life. Eighty million sleeping pills a day — that's how some Americans are saying their prayers at night.

Behind the compulsive habits of many lives is a distinctive philosophy of life. It is the belief that life's satisfactions are found through the stimulation of the senses, by inner excitement, by exploring the world of the self. There is one common factor behind the four major compulsions of alcohol, drugs, gambling, and sex. It is, that pleasurable sensations are all-important and should be sought by any means available. It is the concept that life is satisfying the self. It is slavery to the self.

Many of us don't get caught in the more obvious compulsions of booze and gambling and sexual traps. We satisfy the self with too much food, or with biting tongues that cut someone else apart, or with social attitudes that demand that we belittle people of racial or social class different from our own, in order that we may satisfy our own egos. Jesus frees us from a concept of life addicted to the self. "He breathed on them his Holy Spirit and commanded them to be *his* witnesses."

Jesus gives us freedom in a third area, freedom from fear of the future. We all face unknown futures. Soren Kierkegaard once described anxiety as "the next day." Somewhere in tomorrow stands death. Jesus frees us from fear of death when he says, "You who live and believe in me, even though you die, yet shall you live." We have the promise of the Resurrection. We have a God who is a loving and good God and so we should never be afraid of whatever the future will bring. "Fear not, for behold I bring you good news, unto you is born a Savior, Christ the Lord." Jesus makes us free from the past, from bondage to our present weak egos, from fear of the future.

From death to life — those are not just events described in the Bible — they are happening right here today. The young man from Ohio points the way, "When I met Jesus."

Robert Frost put his finger on the cause of inner bondage to the past, to death. He said, "Something we are withholding left us weak/Until we found out it was ourselves."

The young man from Ohio said, "When I met Jesus it was just like the Bible says, walking from darkness into light, from the land of the dead to the living."